Am

COLLINS

Glasgow & London

First published 1990
Copyright © William Collins Sons & Company Limited
Published by William Collins Sons & Company Limited
Printed in Hong Kong
ISBN 0 00 435769-8

HOW TO USE THIS BOOK

Your Collins Traveller Guide will help you find your way around your chosen destination quickly and easily. It is colour-coded for easy reference:

The blue-coded 'topic' section answers the question 'I would like to see or do something; where do I go and what do I see when I get there?' A simple, clear layout provides an alphabetical list of activities and events, offers you a selection of each, tells you how to get there, what it will cost, when it is open and what to expect. Each topic in the list has its own simplified map, showing the position of each item and the nearest landmark or transport access, for instant orientation. Whether your interest is Architecture or Food you can find all the information you need quickly and simply. Where major resorts within an area require in-depth treatment, they follow the main topics section in alphabetical order.

The red-coded section is a lively and informative gazetteer. In one alphabetical list you can find essential facts about the main places and cultural items - 'What is La Bastille?', 'Who was Michelangelo?' - as well as practical and invaluable travel information. It covers everything you need to know to help you enjoy yourself and get the most out of your time away, from Accommodation through Babysitters, Car Hire, Food, Health, Money, Newspapers, Taxis and Telephones to Zoos.

Cross-references: Type in small capitals - **CHURCHES** - tells you that more information on an item is available within the topic on churches. A-Z in bold - **A-Z** - tells you that more information is available on an item within the gazetteer. Simply look under the appropriate heading. A name in bold - **Holy Cathedral** - also tells you that more information on an item is available in the gazetteer under that particular heading.

Packed full of information and easy to use - you'll always know where you are with your Collins Traveller Guide!

Photography by **Phil Springthorpe**

INTRODUCTION

What is it about Amsterdam that draws over one-and-a-half million visitors each year, a number which puts it fourth to Rome, London and Paris in the league of European tourist attractions?

After all, it is in essence a small city, and it is not spectacular, at least not in the sense of offering sights which impress by their magnificence. Although the capital of The Netherlands, it lacks the kind of civic grandeur commonly associated with capital cities, one explanation for which is the odd fact that the seat of the nation's government is else-where, at The Hague. It has few, if any monuments which can be described as great. Yet you could not possibly say of Amsterdam (to adapt Churchill's comment on Clement Attlee) that it is a modest little place with much to be modest about. Instead you would have to say that, yes, it is unassuming, its buildings mostly bourgeois in spirit rather than patrician, its overall character intimate rather than imposing, and that therein lies a large part of its distinctive charm.

Because Amsterdam does not intimidate, because it is not bewilder-ingly large, because it does not boast vistas or edifices which overawe, you feel physically at ease there, with a sense that everything around you is on a properly human scale. And this feeling of physical ease is immensely enhanced by the city's most striking topographical feature, its 160 canals which add up to 100 km of waterways. Amsterdam is softened and made delightfully picturesque by its canals, as it is by the tall and graceful trees which stand at intervals along them and the many small bridges which curve over them.

There is good reason to take to the canals in one of the glass-roofed boats provided by the several operators of such trips. It is a pleasantly effortless way to see the handsome mansions and warehouses which overlook the principal canals, the majority dating from the 17thC and exemplifying Dutch architecture at its most idiosyncratic and appeal-ing, particularly in the variety of gables. If you make your canal trip after dark, you will have a lovely impression of large, lighted windows, each with enticing hints of civilized living within, shedding a golden radiance over the black water.

As is true of any city, however, the only way really to get the feel of Amsterdam is, of course, by discovering it for yourself. The rewards will be many. Few cities bespeak their history as attractively as Amsterdam,

and in none does contemporary life seem more enjoyable.
Amsterdam's history, though not long, is rich with interest. The sophisticated metropolis of today - the second port of The Netherlands as well as the capital, and a financial centre of world importance - began life as a fishing settlement established around 1225 on the bank of the river Amstel where it joined the river IJ to flow into the Zuider Zee and thence into the North Sea. 50 years later the inhabitants of the expanding settlement built a dam on the Amstel, hence the name 'Amstelledamme' which in due course became 'Amsterdam'. From 1300, when it was first granted a city charter, Amsterdam developed into an ever more thriving port and an increasingly prosperous trading city. The peak of its fortunes came in the 17thC when, as the foremost port and chief city of Holland, it was the hub of the vast maritime empire opened up by Dutch merchants (those of the Dutch East India Company, for example, which was founded in 1602) and the mainspring of the nation's emergence as a world power.

It is a paradox that this city, made by merchants and still seeming at first acquaintance quintessentially bourgeois, should have had a long tradition of liberalism. Amsterdammers were noted in the past not only for their religious toleration but for their respect for freedom of conscience in all matters. This cast of mind is manifest today in the tolerance of the majority of Amsterdammers towards the minority who cultivate alternative styles of life. The policy of the city authorities as regards drugs and prostitution can also be seen as characteristically tolerant, although shrewd might be a more apt description - legalizing soft drugs and corralling prostitutes conspicuously in one area are sensible methods of control. The Red Light District of Amsterdam, which is in the *Walletjes*, the old city centre, provides the now famous spectacle of 'girls' by the hundred brazenly displaying themselves in front rooms which often seem a parody of the bourgeois parlour. The old part of the city also provides, in particular venues, the public performances of live sex which have earned Amsterdam its reputation as a sex capital. The 'live and let live' atmosphere of Amsterdam makes it, in general, a most relaxing place to be in. As you find your way around, you feel not just physically at ease but somehow emotionally at ease as well, untrammelled by convention.

The chances are you will choose to discover the city on foot. Nothing could be more agreeable than strolling beside the Herengracht or the Keizersgracht or the Prinsengracht, the three great semi-circular canals which were built in the 17th C and comprise the celebrated *grachtengordel* (canal girdle). Ambling through the area known as the Jordaan is hardly less of a pleasure: once the French sector of Amsterdam and primarily a working-class district, the Jordaan is now the bohemian quarter of the city, an alluring admixture of lively cafés and restaurants, avant-garde galleries and small bookshops, trendy boutiques and hippy-ish arts-and-crafts shops. Otherwise, you may opt for doing your exploring by bicycle. Hiring one is simple and riding one gives you the satisfying sensation of being an honorary Amsterdammer (one of many engaging facts about Amsterdam is that it has a bicycle count of 540,000 for a population of 750,000). A bicycle ride or two could take you to the Singel canal to see the floating flower market, to the Amstel to see some of the prettiest of Amsterdam's 2800 houseboats, to the historic square known as the Dam to see the somewhat ponderously Baroque Koninklijk Paleis, to the Anne Frank Huis on Prinsengracht, to

Het Rembrandthuis Museum (Rembrandt House) in the old Jewish sector of the city, to Waterlooplein to see the flea market, to the Rijksmuseum to see its magnificent display of paintings by Rembrandt, Vermeer, de Hoogh and other Dutch Masters, to the Van Gogh Museum to see its unparalleled representation of this marvellous artist's work, to the Stedelijk Museum to see its excellent collection of modern and contemporary art, to one of the traditional brown cafés of Amsterdam for a restorative cup of coffee or perhaps a nip of Dutch gin, to … the possibilities in this most seductive of cities seem endless. Whatever the means of transport you decide on, the only thing likely to vex you in Amsterdam is the sheer amount of interesting things to see and pleasurable things to do.

Elizabeth Claridge

GALERIE GAMMA Keizersgracht 429.
• 1130-1730 Tues.-Sat. Tram 1, 2, 5. • Free.
Abstract canvases and contemporary paintings of the canals.

GALERIE HAMER Leliegracht 38.
• 1330-1730 Tues.-Sat. Tram 13, 14, 17. • Free.
A small gallery specializing in naive art.

GALERIE LIEVE HEMEL Vijzelgracht 6-8.
• 1200-1800 Tues.-Sat. Tram 16, 24, 25. • Free.
*Contemporary Dutch realist paintings and sculptures exhibited in
an attractive 17thC house with steep staircases and low ceilings.*

BARBARA FARBER Keizersgracht 265.
• 1200-1800 Tues.-Sat. Tram 13, 14, 17. • Free.
An active promoter of fresh talent, particularly the New York avant-garde.

JURKA Singel 28.
• 1200-1700 Wed.-Sat., 1500-1700 Sun. Tram 1, 2, 5, 13, 17. • Free.
Contemporary paintings and photographs.

GOOIJER GALLERY Prinsengracht 510.
• 1200-1700 Mon.-Sat., 1300-1700 Sun. Tram 1, 2, 5. • Free.
Well-presented modern art. Weekly exhibitions.

DE 3 GRATIEN Weteringstraat 39.
• 1200-1730 Tues.-Fri., 1100-1700 Sat. Tram 6, 7, 16, 24, 25. • Free.
Quite respectable erotic pictures by local artists.

CANON IMAGE CENTRE Leidsestraat 79.
• 1200-1745 Tues.-Fri., 1100-1645 Sat. Tram 1, 2, 5. • Free.
International photography. Superb view of the canals from the upper floors.

AMAZONE GALERIE Singel 72.
• 1200-1745 Tues.-Fri., 1100-1645 Sat. Tram 1, 2, 5, 13, 17. • Free.
Works by female artists and exhibitions on women's issues.

DE DOFFER Runstraat 12.
•1100-0100. Tram 1, 2, 5.
Easy-going little café mostly frequented by students.

FRASCATI Nes 59.
•1000-0100 Mon.-Sat., 1700-0100 Sun. Tram 4, 9, 14, 16, 24, 25.
Elegant decor, reasonably-priced food and a theatre-going clientele.

HOPPE Spui 18.
•1100-0100. Tram 1, 2, 5.
*Amsterdam's most famous brown café (see **A-Z**) and possibly its busiest. Always buzzing with good-humoured conversation.*

PAPENEILAND Prinsengracht 2.
•1100-0100 Mon.-Sat. Bus 18, 22, 44.
*Notable brown café (see **A-Z**). Atmospheric interior and antique decor.*

ORANJERIE Binnen Oranjestraat 15.
•1500-0100 Mon.-Thurs., 1500-0200 Fri. & Sat. Tram 3; Bus 18, 22.
Relaxed and friendly atmosphere. Hollywood posters cover the walls.

DE REIGER Nieuwe Leliestraat 34.
•0900-0100 Sun.-Thurs., 0900-0200 Fri. & Sat. Tram 13, 14, 17.
*One of the most popular Jordaan (see **CITY DISTRICTS**, **WALK 1**, **A-Z**) cafés.*

DE ELANDS Prinsengracht 296.
•1000-0100 Sun.-Thurs., 1000-0200 Fri. & Sat. Tram 13, 14, 17.
Captures the atmosphere of old Amsterdam. A terrace overlooks the canal.

HET MOLENPAD Prinsengracht 653.
•1200-0100 Sun.-Thurs., 1200-0200 Fri. & Sat. Tram 1, 2, 5, 7, 10.
An attractive setting and one of the best café cuisines in the city.

HET HOK Lange Leidsedwarsstraat 134.
•1000-0100 Sun.-Thurs., 1000-0200 Fri. & Sat. Tram 1, 2, 5.
Board games like chess, draughts and backgammon are a popular feature.

AMSTEL RIVER
Tram 6, 7, 9, 10, 14; M Waterlooplein, Weesperplein.
A natural waterway with a more open outlook than the canals, featuring the Magere Brug (see A-Z) and the Carré Theatre (see THEATRE & CINEMA 1).

SINGEL
Tram 4, 9, 14, 16, 24, 25 to Muntplein.
*Innermost of the grachtengordel (see **Canals**). Once the city moat, it now houses the Flower Market (see **Drijvende Bloemenmarkt**). See WALK 3 & 5.*

HERENGRACHT
Tram 1, 2, 5 to Koningsplein.
The 'Gentlemen's Canal', containing some of the grandest merchants' houses, especially between Leidsegracht and Vijzelstraat. See WALK 5.

KEIZERSGRACHT
Tram 13, 14, 17 to Westermarkt.
The 'Emperor's Canal', slightly less grand but still featuring an impressive display of facades and gables. See WALK 5.

PRINSENGRACHT
Tram 13, 14, 17 to Westermarkt.
The 'Prince's Canal', formerly accommodating tradesmen and artisans. Look out for the old warehouses: many are still in use today. See WALK 5.

BROUWERSGRACHT
Tram 3; Bus 18, 22, 44 to Haarlemmerplein.
Some of Amsterdam's prettiest canal views are to be seen along here.

LIJNBAANSGRACHT
Tram 3; Bus 18, 22, 44 to Haarlemmerplein.
Admire the beautiful waterside gardens.

REGULIERSGRACHT
Tram 4, 9, 14 to Rembrandtsplein.
Famous for its view of seven canal bridges in a row. See WALK 5.

MADAME TUSSAUD Kalverstraat 156.
•0900-1900 July-Aug., 1000-1800 Sept.-June.
Tram 1, 2, 4, 5, 9, 14, 16, 24, 25. •f9,50, child f5,50.
*Wax effigies of historical and contemporary figures. Special displays on Rembrandt (see **A-Z**) and Anne Frank (see **MUSEUMS 1**, **A-Z**).*

ARTIS ZOO Plantage Kerklaan 40.
•0900-1700. Tram 7, 9, 14; Bus 56. •f12, child f6.
To be congratulated for keeping its animals (some 6000 in all) in conditions closely resembling their natural habitats.

KINDERMUSEUM TM JUNIOR Linnaeusstraat 2a.
•1300-1530. Tram 9, 14; Bus 22. •f2,50-f5.
Displays and activities on Third World problems, for children aged 6-12.

ZEISS PLANETARIUM Plantage Kerklaan 40.
•0900-1700. Tram 7, 9, 14; Bus 56.
The universe explained in this planetarium in the zoo.

GAASPERPLAS
•0800-dusk. M Gaasperplas; Bus 60, 61, 137, 174.
*Barbecues, picnic areas and a water playground. See **PARKS**.*

MADURODAM Haringkade 175, The Hague.
•0930-2230 Apr.-June, 0930-2300 July-Aug., 0930-1700 Sept., 0930-1300 Oct. Train, bus to The Hague, then Tram 1, 9.
*Miniature town with finely detailed buildings and working models. See **A-Z**.*

DE EFTELING Europaweg 1, Kaatsheuvel.
•1000-1800 Apr.-Oct.
Family leisure park with fairy-tale theme and ingenious thrill-rides. Great fun.

CANAL BOAT TRIP
•Departures every 15 min. Tram 4, 9, 14, 16, 24, 25. •f8 per hr.
A must for every visitor. Boarding points on Prins Hendrikkade, Stadhouderskade, Damrak and Rokin.

NIEUWE KERK Dam Square.
•1100-1600 Mon.-Sat., 1200-1500 Sun. Closed Jan., Feb. Tram 1, 2, 5.
Founded in the 15thC and extensively rebuilt since then. It is still used for state occasions, exhibitions and concerts. See **WALK 2**.

ENGELSE KERK Begijnhof 48.
Tram 1, 2, 4, 5, 9, 24, 25.
Plain Presbyterian church in a tranquil setting. See **WALK 2**, **Begijnhof**.

OUDE KERK Oudekerksplein 23.
•1000-1600 Mon.-Sat. Tram 4, 9, 16, 24, 25. •f1.
Amsterdam's biggest church, and its oldest. See **WALK 4**.

WESTERKERK Prinsengracht 281.
•1000-1600 Mon.-Sat. (May-Sept.). Tram 13, 14, 17.
Adorned by an impressive tower offering a splendid view. See **WALK 1**.

NOORDERKERK Noordermarkt.
Tram 3; Bus 18, 22, 44.
Site of a Monday antiques market and a Saturday bird market. See **WALK 1**.

ZUIDERKERK Zuiderkerkhof, entry at St Antoniesbreestraat 130-132.
•1100-1400 Thurs., Fri., 1100-1600 Sat. (June-Oct.). M Nieuwmarkt.
Amsterdam's first major post-Reformation church.

PORTUGUESE SYNAGOGUE Jonas Daniël Meijerplein.
Tram 9, 14; Bus 31, 56; M Waterlooplein.
A testimony to the influence of the Jewish community in Amsterdam.

ST NICOLAASKERK Prins Hendrikkade 73.
Opposite Centraal Station. Most trams and buses.
Where Sinterklaas (Santa Claus) begins the November festivities. See **WALK 4**.

RONDE LUTHERSE KERK Singel, at Kattengat.
Walking distance from Centraal Station.
Distinctive dome. Now a concert venue and conference centre. See **WALK 5**.

MODERN ARCHITECTURAL DISTRICT, NORTH
Spaarndammerplantsoen, off Zaanstraat. Bus 22, 28.
Three striking housing blocks by Michael de Klerk. See **Architecture***.*

THE JORDAAN
Between Prinsengracht and Lijnbaansgracht. Tram 13, 14, 17.
A picturesque jumble of narrow streets, shops and cafés. See WALK 1*,* **A-Z***.*

THE RED LIGHT DISTRICT
Oudezijds Voorburgwal, Oudezijds Achterburgwal. Tram 4, 9, 16, 24.
The astonishing sights of shamelessly liberal Amsterdam. See WALK 4*,* **A-Z***.*

THE JEWISH QUARTER
Geldersekade to Nieuwe Herengracht. M Nieuwmarkt, Waterlooplein.
The run-down remains of Amsterdam's once-thriving Jewish community.

THE COMMERCIAL DISTRICT
Around Nieuwendijk and Kalverstraat. Tram 1, 2, 4, 5, 9, 16, 24, 25.
Characterized by narrow, bustling pedestrianized streets containing all kinds of shops. See SHOPPING 1 & 3*.*

THE MAIN CANALS
From Brouwersgracht to the Amstel River.
History and commerce intermingle here. Numerous photogenic views.

MUSEUMPLEIN DISTRICT
Tram 2, 3, 5, 6, 7, 10, 12.
Cultural heart of Amsterdam, housing all the main museums. See SQUARES*.*

MODERN ARCHITECTURAL DISTRICT, SOUTH
Vrijheidslaan, P. L. Takstraat, J. Vermeerplein, R. Hartplein. Tram 3, 4, 5.
Exceptional housing blocks from the Amsterdam School. See **Architecture***.*

THE VONDELPARK AREA
Around Overtoom and Willemsparkweg. Tram 1, 2, 5, 6.
Chic shops and elegant mansions surround the park. See PARKS*,* **A-Z***.*

MAZZO Rozengracht 114.
- 2300-0400 Sun.-Thurs., 2300-0500 Fri. & Sat. Tram 13, 14. •f5-f7,50.
Popular with the trendies of the Jordaan (see CITY DISTRICTS, WALK 1, A-Z).

EXIT Reguliersdwarsstraat 42.
- 2200-0400 Sun.-Thurs., 2200-0500 Fri. & Sat. Tram 16, 24. •f5-f7,50.
Same owners as April (see MODERN BARS), *a nearby gay bar. Always busy.*

JULIANA'S Apollolaan 138 (enter on Breitnerstraat).
- 2200-0400 Sun.-Thurs., 2200-0500 Fri. & Sat. Tram 16; Bus 66. •f5.
Stylish up-market disco in the Hilton Hotel.

BOSTON CLUB Kattengat 1.
- 2200-0400 Sun.-Thurs., 2200-0500 Fri. & Sat. Tram 1, 2, 5, 13. •Free.
The Sonesta Hotel's superior disco. Expect to pay heavily for drinks.

ZORBA DE BUDDHA Oudezijds Voorburgwal 216.
- 2100-0200 Sun.-Thurs., 2100-0300 Fri. & Sat. Tram 16, 24. •f5-f10.
Spacious and welcoming disco where drugs are not tolerated.
It was established by followers of the Bhagwan Shree Rajneesh.

MALOE MELO Lijnbaansgracht 160.
- 2200-late Mon.-Sat. Tram 1, 2, 5, 6, 7, 10. •Free.
Rough-and-ready live music club, with the emphasis on R & B.

MELKWEG Lijnbaansgracht 234a.
- 1800-late. Tram 1, 2, 5, 6, 7, 10. •Free.
Slightly oddball disco in a famous multifunctional arts centre.

PARADISO Weteringschans 6-8.
- Opening times vary - check press. Tram 1, 2, 5, 6, 7, 10. •f5-f10.
Another multipurpose venue, this one located in a converted church.

BE-BOP Amstelstraat 2.
- 2200-0400 Thurs., 2200-0500 Fri. & Sat. Tram 4, 9. •f7,50-f10.
American-style decor in an almost overwhelmingly large disco.

De Dam

The Old Zuider Zee

A one-day excursion exploring the coastal towns to the north of Amsterdam and the reclaimed polders of Flevoland.

Leave Amsterdam by the IJ-Tunnel and head north on the N 10 motor-way for six km before turning right onto the N 247.

10 km - Broek in Waterland. A pretty and peaceful village with tiny, neat wooden houses dating from the 17th and 18thC. Everything about the place is proudly maintained in a clean and orderly fashion by the inhabitants. Buildings, gardens, streets, pavements - all are immaculate. Continue on the same road going in the same direction.

13 km - Monnickendam. You are now at the former Zuider Zee (see **IJsselmeer**, **Markermeer**), and the first of many fishing villages visited on this excursion. Smoked eel is a favourite delicacy around here, and smokehouses are still in production in the harbour area. Drive seven km to the east and cross the causeway.

20 km - Marken (see **A-Z**). A trip to this little island is very worthwhile. Many of the locals still wear colourful traditional costumes, adding to the picturesque appeal of the tiny wooden houses. The museum gives an insight into the island's history, and the church contains model fish-ing boats. Retrace your route to the N 247 at Monnickendam, turn right and head north for five km.

32 km - Volendam (see **A-Z**). Sadly the tourist trade has rather spoilt this once much-admired coastal town, but some of the buildings retain their charm. Carry on for one km to the north.

33 km - Edam (see **A-Z**). The town which gave its name to the famous cheese has greater appeal than Volendam. The Kaasmarkt (Cheese Market) is an obvious attraction, but also try to make time to explore the Edams Museum at Damplein 8, which contains many fascinating curios (Apr.-Oct. 1000-1630 Mon.-Sat., 1400-1630 Sun.). Keep going north along the N 247.

50 km - Hoorn. The town gave its name to Cape Horn, which was first rounded by Willem Schouten, a native of the town, in 1616. Two other well-known citizens who were explorers and colonizers in the 17thC were Jan Pieterszoon Coen, who founded Batavia (now Jakarta), and Abel Tasman, who discovered New Zealand. The attractive waterways and buildings of Hoorn are pleasant to explore, and the Westfries

Museum at Rodesteen 1 has many interesting exhibits, although the lack of explanatory labelling may disappoint the visitor (1100-1700 Mon.-Fri., 1400-1700 Sat. & Sun.). Head inland and northwards on the A 7 and turn right after 12 km, following the signs for Medemblik.

64 km - Medemblik. Features a busy harbour filled with countless yachts. The Kasteel Radbout beside the harbour stands on the site of a Frisian castle originally dating from the 8thC, and fortified in the 13thC. The nearby twin villages of Twisk and Opperdoes are extremely picturesque. Continue in an easterly direction along the geometric array of polderland roads and you will find yourself passing through many more such attractive communities.

84 km - Enkhuizen (see **A-Z**). One of the highlights of the trip is the Zuider Zee Museum, a fascinating local history musem. The major attraction - a recreation of a typical Zuider Zee village - is outdoors and only accessible by a special ferry. Allow plenty of time to do this excellent museum justice before enjoying one of those experiences almost unique to the Netherlands - a drive across the sea. The new dike road will carry you the 30 km over the former Zuider Zee to Flevoland.

114 km - Lelystadt. A new town contrasting sharply to the historic towns you have just travelled through. Since the mid-1960s Lelystadt has grown from nothing to a settlement of 55,000 inhabitants. It is a fairly dreary place, but its interest lies in the amazing engineering feat that reclaimed all the surrounding land from the sea. Follow the A 6 and then the A 1 motorways back to Amsterdam (50 km) past acres of rapeseed fields, which are a brilliant yellow in the springtime.

EXCURSION 2

Noord-Holland

A six-hour excursion visiting the major attractions of Noord-Holland.

Either head north from the city centre through the 1J-Tunnel or take the Coentunnel to the west of the city. Turn left, following the signs for Zaandam.

10 km - Zaandam (see **A-Z**). Zaandam and the surrounding towns more or less constitute a sprawling industrial suburb of Amsterdam, but the area is not without its attractions. The Russian Tsar, Peter the Great, visited Zaandam several times between 1697 and 1717 to study Dutch shipbuilding techniques. The modest house where he stayed is situated near the Dam and has been converted into a museum. Continue north along the N 203 trunk road for a short distance before turning off to Zaanse Schans.

12 km - Zaanse Schans (see **A-Z**). This pleasant windmill village, constructed in 17thC style, was opened in 1960. The houses, museums and craft shops give you a real taste of life in bygone times. Rejoin the N 203 going north and look out for the N 244 turn-off just after Wormerveer.

30 km - Alkmaar (see **A-Z**). The famous cheese-making centre. If you leave Amsterdam early enough on a Friday, you can catch the bustle of the Cheese Market in action before it closes at midday. Take the easterly road through Bergen and turn left before Bergen aan Zee.

55 km - Noordhollands Duinreservaat. This protected area of forestry and sand dunes lies to your right as you pass Castricum. Go south from here along the A 9 and A 208 motorways.

65 km - Haarlem (see **A-Z**). The capital of the province of Noord-Holland. Recommended sights include the Franz Hals Museum and the Sint Bavokerk (also know simply as the Grote Kerk), but the numerous little backstreets contain enough quaint shops and picturesque courtyards to make a visit enjoyable just by strolling around. On leaving the town, follow the N 201.

75 km - Zandvoort (see **A-Z**). A popular seaside resort with a long sandy beach and all the amenities you would normally expect including restaurants, cafés, a dolphinarium and a casino. Return to Amsterdam (approx. 30 km) along the N 201 and the A 5 going in a westerly direction.

Tulip Country

A four-hour visit to the bulb fields south west of Amsterdam. Start out early to reach Aalsmeer in time for the Flower Auction.

Take the A 10 and A 4 motorways out of Amsterdam to just past Schiphol (see **Airport**).

16 km - Aalsmeer (see **A-Z**). The wonderful Flower Auction is a must, so try to reach it well before 0900 or you will miss much of the fun. Flowers may remind you of romance, but the mechanized techniques and businesslike atmosphere here will remind you just how important the trade is to the economy of the Netherlands. Leaving Aalsmeer, follow the westward-bound N 201.

30 km - Heemstede. This suburb of Haarlem (see **EXCURSION 2**, **A-Z**) provides an interesting distraction from the tulip fields in the form of the Croquius Expo at Croquiusdijk 27, a fascinating exhibition of old land-reclamation techniques. The N 208 leading south from the town will take you through the *bloembollenstreek*, the main area for bulb cultivation in the Netherlands. During April and May you can enjoy the sight of quite breathtaking expanses of colour.

38 km - Hillegom. This, along with the following two destinations, is one of the main centres for tulip growing. Here you can admire the demonstration garden at Treslong, which contains a quite astonishing number of bulb varieties. Continue along the same road for a further four km.

42 km - Lisse. Home of the famous Keukenhof Exhibition (see **A-Z**). The acres of flowerbeds, greenhouses and gardens are a stunning sight. For background information on bulb cultivation, visit the museum at Heereweg 219.

46 km - Sassenheim. This town marks the southernmost edge of the tulip country, and from here you can return quickly to Amsterdam on the A 44 and A 4 motorways. Alternatively you could make your way back to the city in a more leisurely fashion along the network of narrow roads which crisscross the bulb fields.

DE BLINCKER St Barberenstraat 7.
•1000-0100. Tram 4, 9, 14, 16, 24, 25.
Split-level interior and ultra-modern decor. Late in the evening it's packed with theatre-goers from the adjacent Frascati Theatre.

OBLOMOW Reguliersdwarsstraat 40.
•1300-0100 Mon.-Thurs., 1300-0200 Fri. & Sat., 1600-0100 Sun.
Tram 1, 2, 5.
*Chic and extremely comfortable bar which is the antithesis of the brown café (see **A-Z**).*

L'OPERA Rembrandtsplein, at Bakkersstraat.
•1300-0100 Mon.-Thurs., 1300-0200 Fri. & Sat. Tram 4, 9, 14.
Decorated in the style of a Parisian brasserie of the 1930s.

APRIL Reguliersdwarsstraat 37.
•1300-0100 Mon.-Thurs., 1300-0200 Fri. & Sat. Tram 1, 2, 5.
Gay bar, busy in the evenings but retaining a relaxed atmosphere.

CAFÉ DE BAST Huidenstraat 19.
•1130-2030 Mon.-Sat., 1700-2030 Sun. Tram 1, 2, 5.
Smart pine decor and a moderately-priced menu.

HARRY'S AMERICAN BAR Spuistraat 285.
•1700-0100 Mon.-Thurs., 1700-0200 Fri. & Sat., 2200-0100 Sun.
Tram 1, 2, 5.
The name describes the style of this popular spot. Cocktails are the speciality of the house.

BIM CAFÉ Oudeschans 73-79.
•2000-0200 Mon.-Thurs., 2000-0300 Fri. & Sat. Tram 9, 14.
Situated in the Bimhuis Jazz Centre.

WILDSCHUT Roelof Hartplein 1.
•0900-0100. Tram 3, 5, 12, 24.
Art Deco cinema fittings create a pleasant atmosphere.

DAM NATIONAL MONUMENT Dam Square.
Tram 4, 9, 16, 24, 25.
Memorial to the dead of the Second World War. See **WALK 2**, **Dam Square**.

MUNTTOREN Muntplein.
Tram 4, 9, 14, 16, 24, 25.
Built in 1622 on the site of one of the city's oldest gates. See **A-Z**.

HET LIEVERDJE Spui.
Tram 1, 2, 5.
Statue of a street urchin, a rallying point for 1960s radicals. See **WALK 3**.

AMERICAN HOTEL Leidsekade 97.
Tram 1, 2, 5, 6, 7, 10.
This protected building is a long-standing favourite with writers and artists.

TUSCHINSKI CINEMA Reguliersbreestraat 26.
Tram 4, 9, 14, 16, 24, 25.
A fantastical building with remarkable interiors dating from 1921. Cinema 1 is the most ornate. See **THEATRE & CINEMA 1**, **WALK 5**.

GAY MONUMENT Westermarkt.
Tram 13, 14, 17; Bus 21, 67.
Dedicated in 1985 to homosexuals who suffered at the hands of the Nazis.

BEGIJNHOF Spui.
Tram 4, 9, 14, 16, 24, 25.
Quiet courtyard in a protected Beguine convent. See **WALK 2 & 3**, **A-Z**.

SCHREIERSTOREN Geldersekade.
Walking distance from Centraal Station. Most trams and buses.
Legendary site of tearful farewells in medieval times. See **WALK 4**, **A-Z**.

DE DOKWERKER Jonas Daniël Meijerplein.
Tram 9, 14; Bus 31, 56; M Waterlooplein.
Commemorates the 1941 dockworkers' strike in support of oppressed Jews.

HET IJ

Nederlands Scheepvaart-museum

Zeeburgerdijk

Middenweg

Linnaeusstraat

Prins Hendrikkade

Mauritskade

OUDESCHANS

Wibautstraat

Weesperstraat

AMSTEL

Centraal Station

Van Woustraat

O. VOORBURGWAL

SINGEL GRACHT

Rokin

Damrak

Vijzelgracht

Ceintuurbaan

Overholland Museum

SINGEL GRACHT

HEREN GRACHT

KEIZERS GRACHT

PRINSEN GRACHT

Hobbemakade

Rozengracht

Nassaukade

V. Baerlestraat

Haarlemmerweg

Stedelijk Museum

Ann Frank's House

Royal Palace

Jan van Galenstraat

Rijksmuseum

Van Gogh Museum

Overtoom

VONDELPARK

RIJKSMUSEUM Stadhouderskade 42.
•1000-1700 Tues.-Sat., 1300-1700 Sun.
Tram 3, 5, 6, 7, 10; Bus 26, 65, 66, 170, 179. •f6,50 or Museumcard.
Internationally renowned. The Netherlands' major museum of art, housing works by all the great masters of the Golden Age. See **A-Z**.

VAN GOGH MUSEUM Paulus Potterstraat 7.
•1000-1700 Tues.-Sat., 1300-1700 Sun.
Tram 2, 3, 5, 12, 16; Bus 26, 65, 66, 170, 179. •f6,50 or Museumcard.
Offers an insight into the great Dutch artist and his contemporaries through letters and documents as well as paintings and drawings. See **WALK 3**, **A-Z**.

STEDELIJK MUSEUM Paulus Potterstraat 13.
•1100-1700. Tram 2, 3, 5, 12, 16; Bus 26, 65, 66, 170, 179.
•f5 or Museumcard.
Modern and contemporary paintings, sculptures and photographs. See **A-Z**.

OVERHOLLAND MUSEUM Museumplein 4.
•1000-1700 Tues.-Sat., 1300-1700 Sun. Tram 2, 3, 5, 12, 16. •f5.
Modern and contemporary art. Frequently holds special exhibitions.

ANNE FRANK'S HOUSE Prinsengracht 263.
•0900-1700 Mon.-Sat., 1000-1700 Sun. Tram 13, 14, 17. •f5.
Concealed behind a sliding bookcase is the attic where Anne wrote her diary as she and her family hid from the Nazis. See **A-Z**.

ROYAL PALACE (KONINKLIJK PALEIS) Dam Square.
•1230-1600 June-Aug. Tram 1, 2, 4, 5, 9, 13, 14, 16, 17, 24, 25. •f1.
Attractions include opulent interiors and Louis Napoleon's private collection of furnishings. See **OFFICIAL BUILDINGS**, **WALK 2**, **A-Z**.

NEDERLANDS SCHEEPVAARTMUSEUM Kattenburgerplein 1.
•1000-1700 Tues.-Sat., 1300-1700 Sun. Bus 22, 28.
•f5 or Museumcard.
The maritime history of the Netherlands impressively presented in a building which formerly served as the Admiralty arsenal.

HET IJ

Centraal
Station

Damrak

Prins Hendrikkade

O Z VOORBURGWAL

Joods
Historisch
Museum

Kromhout Werfmuseum

Zeeburgerdijk

Middenweg

Linnaeusstraat

Willet-Holthuysen
Museum

Mauritskade

Weesperstraat

Weesperstraat

Wibautstraat

AMSTEL

Van Woustraat

GRACHT

Vijzelgracht

SINGEL

Fodor

Ceintuurbaan

Hokin

SINGEL

HEREN GRACHT

KEIZERS GRACHT

PRINSEN GRACHT

Rozengracht

Nassaukade

Hobbemakade

V Baerlestraat

Haarlemmerweg

Jan van Galenstraat

Amstelkring
Museum

Amsterdams
Historisch
Museum

Bijbels
Museum

Allard Pierson
Museum

Overtoom

VONDELPARK

AMSTERDAMS HISTORISCH MUSEUM Kalverstraat 92.
•1000-1700 Tues.-Sat., 1300-1700 Sun. Tram 1, 2. •f5 or Museumcard.
Exhibits reflecting the social, commercial and political history of the city.

WILLET-HOLTHUYSEN MUSEUM Herengracht 605.
•1000-1700 Tues.-Sat., 1300-1700 Sun. Tram 4, 9. •f2 or Museumcard.
Evocative recreation of the interior of a typical 17th-18thC canal house.

ALLARD PIERSON MUSEUM Oude Turfmarkt 127.
•1000-1700 Tues.-Fri., 1300-1700 Sat. & Sun.
Tram 4, 9, 14, 16, 24. •f3.
Archeological finds from ancient Egypt and the classical world.

BIJBELS MUSEUM Herengracht 366.
•1000-1700 Tues.-Sat., 1300-1700 Sun. Tram 1, 2. •f3 or Museumcard.
Interesting displays on the Bible and its history, in a superb 17thC house.

JOODS HISTORISCH MUSEUM Jonas Daniël Meijerplein 2-4.
•1000-1700. Tram 9; M Waterlooplein. •f5 or Museumcard.
Jewish history and art in Dutch society from the 16thC onwards.

KROMHOUT WERFMUSEUM Hoogte Kadijk 147.
•1000-1600 Mon.-Sat., 1300-1600 Sun. Bus 18, 22. •f3.
*A former shipyard which escaped closure and demolition in 1970 by
conversion into a museum-cum-repair yard.*

AMSTELKRING MUSEUM Oudezijds Voorburgwal 40.
•1000-1700 Mon.-Sat., 1300-1700 Sun. Tram 4, 9, 16, 24, 25.
•f3,50 or Museumcard.
*Known as 'Our Dear Lord in the Attic', this was formerly a secret place of
worship for Catholics. Well worth visiting. See **WALK 4**.*

FODOR Keizersgracht 609.
•1100-1700. Tram 16, 24, 25.
•Admission varies with exhibitions. Museumcard accepted.
Exhibitions of modern works of art, mainly by Dutch artists.

NEDERLANDS THEATER INSTITUUT Herengracht 168.
•1100-1700 Tues.-Sun. Tram 13, 14, 17. •f3 or Museumcard.
The history of the theatre, including reconstructions of stage sets.

NEDERLANDS FILMMUSEUM Vondelpark 3.
•1000-1700 Tues.-Fri., 1300-1700 Sat. & Sun. Tram 1, 2, 3, 5, 6.
•f2,50 or Museumcard.
Ephemera, documents and equipment reflecting the history of the cinema.

HET REMBRANDTHUIS Jodenbreestraat 4-6.
•1000-1700 Mon.-Sat., 1300-1700 Sun. Tram 9. •f3 or Museumcard.
250 sketches and etchings by Rembrandt (see A-Z) displayed in the house where he lived during the 1640s and 1650s.

NINT TECHNOLOGIE MUSEUM Tolstraat 129.
•1000-1700 Mon.-Fri., 1200-1700 Sat. & Sun. Tram 4. •f6.
Working machines and models which make science and technology fun.

TROPENMUSEUM Linnaeusstraat 2.
•1000-1700 Mon.-Fri., 1200-1700 Sat. & Sun. Tram 9.
•f5 or Museumcard.
Aspects of Third World life, especially in former Dutch colonies such as Indonesia. Next door is the Kindermuseum (see CHILDREN).

HORTUS BOTANICUS Plantage Middenlaan 2.
•0900-1600 Mon.-Fri., 1100-1600 Sat. & Sun. Tram 9, 14. •f3.
A wide variety of exotic tropical plants.

AVIODOME Schiphol Airport.
•1000-1700 Tues.-Sun. (Nov.-Mar.). Train, bus to Schiphol. •f5,50.
The role of the Netherlands in aviation history, with aircraft exhibits.

SIX COLLECTION Amstel 218.
•1000-1200, 1400-1600 Mon.-Fri. (summer), 1000-1200 Mon.-Fri. (winter). Tram 4, 9, 14. •Free admission slip from Rijksmuseum.
A fine collection of Dutch Old Masters.

SCHRIFTMUSEUM University Library, Singel 425.
•1000-1300, 1400-1630 Mon.-Fri. Tram 1, 2, 5. •Free.
The evolution of handwriting through the ages, from ancient clay tablets to contemporary letters.

GEMEENTEARCHIEF Amsteldijk 67.
•0845-1645 Mon.-Fri., 0900-1215 Sat. Tram 3, 4. •Free.
Amsterdam's municipal archives. On display are posters, photographs and ephemera to do with the history of the city.

GEOLOGISCH MUSEUM Nieuwe Prinsengracht 130.
•0900-1700 Mon.-Fri. Tram 6, 7, 9, 10. •f3 or Museumcard.
Minerals, ores and fossils from various countries around the world. Largely of specialist appeal.

STICHTING VAN LOON Keizersgracht 672.
•1000-1700 Mon. only. Tram 16, 24, 25. •f5.
House museum containing the Van Loon family's interesting collection of paintings and objets d'art.

SPAARPOTTENMUSEUM Raadhuisstraat 20.
•1300-1600 Mon.-Fri. Tram 13, 14, 17. •f1 or Museumcard.
A highly unusual museum (ideal for children) exhibiting a remarkable collection of money boxes - 12,000 in all! See **WALK 2.**

MULTATULI MUSEUM Korsjespoortsteeg 20.
•1000-1700 Tues. (other days by appointment only).
Tram 1, 2, 5. •Free.
Small but fascinating museum concerned with the Dutch author who attacked the colonial bourgeoisie of the 19thC.

VERZETSMUSEUM Lekstraat 63.
•1000-1700 Tues.-Fri., 1300-1700 Sat. & Sun. Tram 4, 12, 25.
•f5 or Museumcard.
The history of the Dutch Resistance during the Second World War. An imaginative evocation of the atmosphere of the time.

OFFICIAL BUILDINGS

GENERAL POST OFFICE Nieuwezijds Voorburgwal 182.
•0830-1800 Mon.-Fri. (2030 Thurs.), 0900-1200 Sat.
Tram 1, 2, 5, 13, 17.
Remarkable turreted building by P. J. H. Cuypers (1908). See **Architecture**.

BEURS (STOCK EXCHANGE) Beursplein, off Damrak.
Tram 4, 9, 16, 24, 25.
Innovative design by the influential architect Hendrik P. Berlage. Nowadays stages occasional exhibitions and recitals. See **WALK 2**, **Architecture**.

CENTRAAL STATION Stationsplein.
Most trams and buses.
Another grandiose design by Cuypers. Constructed in the late 19thC on an artificial island. See **WALK 2 & 4**, **Architecture**.

STADHUIS Oudezijds Voorburgwal 197-199.
Tram 4, 9, 14, 16, 24, 25.
The Town Hall. A modern construction built on the site of a private hotel.

RAI Europaplein.
Tram 4; Bus 8, 15, 60.
One of the biggest exhibition and conference centres in the world.

CONCERTGEBOUW Van Baerlestraat 98.
Tram 3, 5, 12, 16.
Magnificent acoustics contribute greatly to the worldwide reputation for excellence enjoyed by this concert hall. See **THEATRE & CINEMA 1**, **A-Z**.

ROYAL PALACE (KONINKLIJK PALEIS) Dam Square.
•1230-1600 June-Aug. Tram 1, 2, 4, 5, 9, 13, 14, 16, 17, 24, 25. •f1.
Built in the 17thC as the Town Hall, and converted into a palace in 1808 by the Emperor Louis Napoleon. See **MUSEUMS 1**, **WALK 2**, **A-Z**.

MUNICIPAL LIBRARY Roelof Hartplein 6.
Tram 3, 5, 12.
A fine example of the style of the Amsterdam School. See **Architecture**.

VONDELPARK Stadhouderskade.
•0800-dusk. Tram 1, 2, 3, 5, 6, 12.
The city's most central large park, famous for hippy happenings during the 1960s. 120 acres of lawns, flowerbeds and lakes. See **CITY DISTRICTS**, **A-Z**.

AMSTELPARK Europaboulevard.
•0800-dusk. Bus 8, 49, 60, 157, 173.
Attractions include a maze, an attractive garden and a miniature railway.

AMSTERDAMSE BOS Amstelveenseweg.
•0800-dusk. Bus 170, 171, 172.
The largest park in Amsterdam, with facilities for horse riding, cycling, water sports, tennis, picnicking and camping.

GAASPERPLAS
•0800-dusk. M Gaasperplas; Bus 60, 61, 137, 174.
Water playground with sporting facilities and amenities for barbecues and camping. See **CHILDREN**.

SARPHATIPARK Ceintuurbaan.
•0800-dusk. Tram 3.
A small, pretty park with well-tended flowerbeds and pleasant aspects. Situated in the Old South.

OOSTERPARK Linnaeusstraat.
•0800-dusk. Tram 3, 6, 9, 14.
A restful spot, convenient for the Tropenmuseum (see **MUSEUMS 3***).*

BEATRIXPARK Diepenbrockstraat.
•0800-dusk. Tram 4; Bus 60, 85, 87.
A pleasant area with ponds and waterways situated close to the RAI (see **OFFICIAL BUILDINGS***) and the 1933 Remonstrants Church.*

REMBRANDTPARK Postjesweg.
•0800-dusk. Bus 18, 19, 64.
Extensive park with large artificial lakes and waterways.

Budget

KEUKEN VAN 1870 Spuistraat 4.
●1100-2000 Mon.-Fri., 1100-2100 Sat. & Sun. Tram 1, 2, 5.
Simple Dutch food, basic surroundings and absolutely rock-bottom prices.

DE BLAUWE HOLLANDER Leidsekruisstraat 28.
●1700-2200. Tram 1, 2, 5.
Generous portions of hearty Dutch stews are a speciality.

DE BELHAMEL Brouwersgracht 60 (entry Binnen Wieringerstraat).
●1200-2400 Tues.-Sun. Bus 18, 22.
Surprisingly good international cuisine at reasonable prices, served in a convivial atmosphere.

DE EENHOORN Tweede Egelantiersdwarsstraat 6.
●1730-2300 Wed.-Sun. Tram 13, 14, 17.
The rooftop terrace is a special attraction during summer. Extensive menu.

PIET DE LEEUW Noorderstraat 11.
●1200-2400 Mon.-Fri., 1000-0100 Sat. & Sun. Tram 16, 24, 25.
Steakhouse also famed for its beef casseroles.

LAND VAN WALEM Keizersgracht 449.
●0900-0100 Mon.-Sat., 1000-0100 Sun. Tram 1, 2, 5.
Fashionable restaurant with a terrace overlooking the canal.

PANCAKE BAKERY Prinsengracht 191.
●1200-2200. Tram 13, 14, 17.
Delicious pancakes with a wide selection of sweet and savoury fillings.

HAESJE CLAES Nieuwezijds Voorburgwal 320.
●1200-2200. Tram 4, 9, 16, 24, 25.
Dutch and other continental dishes. Exceptionally good value.

BOJO Lange Leidsedwarsstraat 51.
●1700-0200 Sun.-Thurs., 1700-0530 Fri. & Sat. Tram 1, 2, 5.
Inexpensive Indonesian cuisine. Great for hungry late-night revellers.

Moderate

CAFÉ AMERICAIN Leidsekade 97.
•1100-2400. Tram 1, 2, 5, 6, 7, 10.
International cuisine in the famous American Hotel (see MONUMENTS*).*

LE PECHEUR Reguliersdwarsstraat 32.
•1200-2400 Mon.-Fri., 1700-2400 Sat. & Sun. Tram 1, 2, 5.
Elegant seafood restaurant offering fresh, inventive dishes.

LUCIUS Spuistraat 247.
•1730-2300. Tram 13, 14, 17.
Fish and seafood specialities served in an attractive setting.

INTERMEZZO Herenstraat 28.
•1730-2200 Mon.-Fri., 1800-2230 Sat. & Sun. Tram 1, 2, 5.
French-Dutch cuisine and a refined atmosphere.

RUM RUNNERS Prinsengracht 277.
•1200-2300 Sun.-Thurs., 1200-2400 Fri. & Sat. Tram 13, 14, 17.
A large, noisy eatery serving Caribbean dishes. Live music on Sundays.

CANECAO RIO Reguliersdwarsstraat 8.
•1200-1500, 1700-2400 Mon.-Sat., 1700-2400 Sun. Tram 1, 2, 5.
South American food. The caipirinhas *(cocktails) are recommended.*

THE TANDOOR Leidseplein 19.
•1300-1500, 1730-2330 Tues.-Sun., 1730-2330 Mon. Tram 1, 2, 5.
Pleasant atmosphere. Good tandoori dishes and many other Asian specialities.

SAMA SEBO Hobbemastraat 19.
•1200-1400, 1800-2200 Mon.-Sat. Tram 1, 2, 5.
Famous Indonesian restaurant. Trendy setting and reasonable prices.

SLUIZER Utrechtsestraat 43-45.
•1100-2400 Mon.-Fri., 1700-2400 Sat. & Sun. Tram 4.
Two restaurants offering Dutch cuisine and seafood.

Café Americain

PALLADIUM

Expensive

BRASSERIE VAN BAERLE Van Baerlestraat 158.
- 1200-2300 Mon.-Fri., 1000-2300 Sat. & Sun. Tram 2, 3, 5.
Elegant decor, innovative cuisine, charming and attentive service.

D'VIJFF VLIEGHEN Spuistraat 294 (enter by Vijff Vlieghenweeg).
- 1700-2400. Tram 1, 2, 5.
Traditional Dutch dishes served in traditional Dutch surroundings.

VALENTIJN Kloveniersburgwal 6.
- 1200-1500, 1700-2300 Wed.-Sun., 1700-2300 Mon. & Tues.
Tram 4, 9, 14, 16, 24, 25.
High-quality French cooking and an interesting menu.

DYNASTY Reguliersdwarsstraat 30.
- 1700-2300. Tram 1, 2, 5.
Cantonese haute cuisine. Sumptuous decor.

DE OESTERBAR Leidseplein 10.
- 1200-2400. Tram 1, 2, 5.
*One of the very best seafood restaurants in town, overlooking the busy
Leidseplein (see SQUARES, A-Z).*

DE KERSENTUIN Dijsselhofplantsoen 7.
- 1200-1500, 1800-2400 Mon.-Fri., 1800-2400 Sat.
Tram 16; Bus 66.
*Luxurious and extremely exclusive restaurant in the five-star Garden Hotel.
Serves nouvelle cuisine.*

SAUNA DECO Herengracht 117.
- 1700-late Tues.-Sun. Tram 1, 2, 5, 13, 17.
Dine in style in Art Deco surroundings after having a relaxing sauna.

DIKKER & THIJS Prinsengracht 444.
- Evenings only Mon.-Sat. Tram 1, 2, 5.
*Classic restaurant with old-fashioned attentive service and well-prepared
continental dishes.*

Department Stores

DE BIJENKORF Damrak 90.
•1100-1800 Mon., 0930-1800 Tues.-Fri. (2100 Thurs.), 0900-1700 Sat.
Tram 4, 9, 16, 24, 25.
The biggest, and arguably the best, department store in Amsterdam. Check out the sales on the ground floor. See **WALK 2.**

MAISON DE BONNETERIE Kalverstraat 183/Nieuwezijds Voorburgwal 140.
•1300-1730 Mon., 0915-1730 Tues.-Fri. (2100 Thurs.), 0915-1700 Sat.
Tram 4, 9, 16, 24, 25.
Elegant and pricey store with a range of good-quality classical clothing. Rather conservative.

METZ & CO. Keizersgracht 455.
•1100-1800 Mon., 0930-1800 Tues.-Fri. (2100 Thurs.), 0930-1700 Sat.
Tram 1, 2, 5.
Ideal for gifts, prints and furnishings. The sixth-floor coffee shop has an excellent view over the canals.

VROOM EN DREESMAN Kalverstraat 201.
•1100-1800 Mon., 0930-1800 Tues.-Fri. (2100 Thurs.), 0900-1700 Sat.
Tram 4, 9, 16, 24, 25.
Worth visiting, particularly for the extensive souvenir department and the food hall.

PEEK EN CLOPPENBURG Dam Square.
•1100-1800 Mon., 0930-1800 Tues.-Fri. (2100 Thurs.), 0900-1700 Sat.
Tram 4, 9, 16, 24, 25.
Mainstream store good for middle-of-the-range clothing for all members of the family.

HEMA Nieuwendijk 174-176.
•1100-1800 Mon., 0930-1800 Tues.-Fri. (2100 Thurs.), 0900-1700 Sat.
Tram 4, 9, 16, 24, 25.
One of the biggest branches of this general-goods chain store which is practically a national institution.

Books & Records

ART BOOK Prinsengracht 645.
•1300-1800 Mon., 0900-1800 Tues.-Sat. Tram 16, 24, 25.
A wide selection of books on art and related subjects.

ATHENAEUM Spui 14-16.
•1000-1800 Mon., 0900-1800 Tues.-Fri., 0900-1700 Sat. Tram 1, 2, 5.
General bookshop, with a newsagent selling international publications next door. See **WALK 3.**

SOUND OF THE FIFTIES Prinsengracht 669.
•0930-1800 Mon.-Sat. Tram 1, 2, 5.
New and second-hand records, with the emphasis on American nostalgia.

MARTYRIUM Van Baerlestraat 170.
•1000-1800 Mon., 0900-1800 Tues.-Fri., 0900-1700 Sat. Tram 3, 5, 12.
The best bookshop in this elegant part of town.

ALLERT DE LANGE Damrak 62.
•1300-1800 Mon., 0900-1800 Tues.-Thurs., 0900-1700 Sat. Tram 4, 9.
Excellent selection of maps and guides as well as books.

BOUDISQUE Haringpakkersteeg 10-18.
•1300-1800 Mon., 1000-1700 Tues.-Sat. Tram 4, 9, 16, 24, 25.
Caters for every taste in contemporary music. Good for unusual imports.

NIEUWE MUSICKHANDEL Leidsestraat 50.
•1300-1800 Mon., 0900-1800 Tues.-Fri., 0900-1700 Sat. Tram 1, 2, 5.
Classical records, tapes and compact discs. Also sells concert tickets.

BROEKMANS EN VAN POPPEL Van Baerlestraat 92-94.
•1000-1800 Mon., 0900-1800 Tues.-Fri., 0900-1700 Sat. Tram 3, 5.
Specializes in classical and orchestral music.

JAZZ INN Vijzelgracht 9.
•1230-1730 Mon., 1100-1800 Tues.-Fri., 1000-1700 Sat. Tram 16, 24.
Traditional and contemporary jazz.

Clothes

MAC & MAGGIE Kalverstraat 53 & 172.
•1300-1700 Mon., 0900-1800 Tues.-Fri., 0900-1700 Sat. Tram 4, 9, 14.
Two branches of a nationwide chain selling moderately-priced casual wear.

SISSY BOY Kalverstraat 210.
•1300-1700 Mon., 0900-1800 Tues.-Fri., 0900-1700 Sat. Tram 4, 9, 14.
Sport and leisure clothing.

SACHA Kalverstraat 20 & 161.
•1300-1800 Mon., 0900-1800 Tues.-Fri., 0900-1700 Sat. Tram 4, 9, 14.
Youthful, stylish footwear at reasonable prices.

DR ADAMS Pieter Cornelisz Hooftstraat 90.
•1300-1800 Mon., 0900-1800 Tues.-Fri., 0900-1700 Sat. Tram 2, 3, 5.
Up-market modern and designer shoes.

PAUW Van Baerlestraat 48, 66, 72, & 90.
•1300-1800 Mon., 0900-1800 Tues.-Fri., 0900-1700 Sat. Tram 2, 3, 5.
Fairly exclusive selection of designer clothing. The branch at No. 48 has children's clothes.

VIVALEI Pieter Cornelisz Hooftstraat 94.
•1300-1800 Mon., 0900-1800 Tues.-Fri., 0900-1700 Sat. Tram 2, 3, 5.
Quality footwear. Also has a good children's department.

ANNEKE VELDMAN Hartenstraat 30.
•1100-1800 Mon.-Fri., 1100-1700 Sat. Tram 13, 14, 17.
Clothes and jewellery from the '50s.

PUCK & HANS Rokin 66.
•1100-1800 Mon., 0930-1800 Tues.-Fri., 0930-1700 Sat. Tram 4, 9, 14.
Well-established in fashion circles. Carries Parisian and own designer labels.

ZIPPER Huidenstraat 7.
•1300-1800 Mon., 0930-1800 Tues.-Fri., 1100-1800 Sat. Tram 1, 2, 5.
Specialist in second-hand American classics.

Gifts

RIVET Elandsgracht 69.
• 1200-1700 Wed.-Sat. (1400-1700 Thurs.). Tram 10, 17.
Leather goods - some imported, some designed in-house.

P. G. C. HAJENIUS Rokin 94-96.
• 0900-1800 Mon.-Fri., 0900-1700 Sat. Tram 4, 9, 14, 16, 24, 25.
Tobacco and smokers' accessories. (The Netherlands is famous for its cigars and hand-rolling tobacco.)

WITTE TANDENWINKEL Runstraat 5.
• 1300-1800 Mon., 1000-1800 Tues.-Sat. Tram 1, 2, 5.
Everything for healthy teeth, including jokey items like whisky toothpaste.

DECORATIVA Herenstraat 27.
• 0830-1800. Tram 1, 2, 5, 13, 17.
One of the prettiest window displays in town. Sells flowers and antiques.

POL'S POTTEN Herenstraat 30.
• 1030-1800 Mon.-Fri., 1030-1700 Sat. Tram 1, 2, 5, 13, 17.
Pots, jars and other terracotta items.

'T CURIOSA WINKELTJE Prinsengracht 228.
• 1000-1730 Tues.-Fri., 1000-1700 Sat. Tram 13, 14, 17.
Charmingly cramped gift shop with a delightful selection of curiosities.

DITJES EN DATJES Utrechtsestraat 53.
• 1100-1800 Tues.-Fri., 1100-1700 Sat. Tram 4.
Household gifts and bric-a-brac.

SUNNY HOME Beethovenstraat 10.
• 0900-1800 Tues.-Fri., 1000-1700 Sat. Tram 5.
Modern and designer goods for the home.

POPPENDOKTOR KRAMER Reestraat 20.
• 1000-1800 Tues.-Fri., 1000-1700 Sat. Tram 13, 14, 17.
Huge collection of toys, dolls and puppets, some of them antique.

SQUARES

DAM SQUARE
Tram 1, 2, 4, 5, 9, 16, 24, 25.
*The bustling heart of the city, overlooked by the Royal Palace (see **OFFICIAL BUILDINGS, MUSEUMS 1, A-Z**) and the Nieuwe Kerk (see **CHURCHES**). Often crammed with all kinds of street entertainments. See **WALK 2, A-Z**.*

LEIDSEPLEIN
Tram 1, 2, 5, 7, 10.
*One of the city's major nightlife centres - teeming with cinemas, theatres, restaurants and clubs. See **A-Z**.*

REMBRANDTSPLEIN
Tram 4, 9, 14.
*The statue of the great artist (see **Rembrandt**) is surrounded by cafés, restaurants and topless bars. See **WALK 5, A-Z**.*

MUNTPLEIN
Tram 4, 9, 14, 16, 24, 25.
*Beside the Drijvende Bloemenmarkt (see **A-Z**) and straddling the water-ways. Site of the Munttoren (see **MONUMENTS, WALK 3 & 5, A-Z**).*

SPUI
Tram 1, 2, 5.
*The Café Hoppe (see **CAFÉS, Brown Cafés**) and the Begijnhof (see **MONUMENTS, A-Z**) are two of this busy junction's main attractions. Relax in one of them and watch the world go by. See **WALK 3**.*

WATERLOOPLEIN
Tram 9, 14; M Waterlooplein.
*The heart of the Jewish Quarter (see **CITY DISTRICTS**) and home of the Flea Market (see **A-Z**).*

MUSEUMPLEIN
Tram 3, 5, 12.
*The major museums (see **MUSEUMS 1**) are surrounded by the exclusive shopping streets of P. C. Hooftstraat, Beethovenstraat and Van Baerlestraat.*

CONCERTGEBOUW Van Baerlestraat 98.
Tram 3, 5, 12, 16. •f15-f50.
Internationally renowned concert hall with superb acoustics. Occasionally features rock as well as classical music. See **OFFICIAL BUILDINGS**, **A-Z**.

MUZIEKTHEATER Waterlooplein.
Tram 9, 14; M Waterlooplein. •f20-f50.
A new opera house (opened 1986) offering the best in theatre and dance.

TUSCHINSKI CINEMA Reguliersbreestraat 26.
Tram 4, 9, 14, 16, 24, 25. •f5-f15.
Six screens mostly showing international mainstream films in a building which is itself a work of art. See **MONUMENTS**, **WALK 5**.

CARRÉ THEATRE Amstel 115-125.
Tram 4; M Weesperplein. •f20-f50.
Amsterdam's answer to Broadway - this theatre specializes in presenting major popular musicals.

STADSSCHOUWBURG Leidseplein 26.
Tram 1, 2, 5. •f10-f30.
A famous theatrical centre. Excellent performances of dance and operatic productions.

CINEAC Reguliersbreestraat 31.
Tram 4, 9, 14, 16, 24, 25. •f5-f15.
Has the same owners as the nearby Tuschinski cinema. Programmes consist mainly of art movies.

BELLEVUE Leidsekade 90.
Tram 1, 2, 5. •f15-f20.
Frequently stages English-language theatre productions.

DE KLEINE KOMEDIE Amstel 56.
Tram 4, 9, 14, 16, 24, 25. •f15-f20.
Satirical revues and comedies, often performed in English.

THE CITY Kleine Gartmanplantsoen 13-25.
Tram 1, 2, 5, 6, 7, 10. •f5-f15.
Multi-screen complex in an Art Deco building.

ALFA Hirschgebouw, Kleine Gartmanplantsoen.
Tram 1, 2, 5, 6, 7, 10. •f5-f15.
Shows a variety of mainstream international films.

ALHAMBRA Weteringschans 134.
Tram 4. •f5-f15.
Two screens and a constantly changing programme.

MICKERY THEATRE Rozengracht 117.
Tram 13, 14, 17. •f15-f20.
An adventurous and fairly experimental theatre.

SHAFFY THEATRE Keizersgracht 324.
Tram 1, 2, 5. •f10-f15.
Four auditoriums where anything can happen: from mime to drama, to dance, to circuses. Audience participation is often expected, so be prepared to join in. See **WALK 5.**

ENGLISH SPEAKING THEATRE Rokin 52.
Tram 4, 9, 14, 16, 24, 25.
The company has no permanent venue for performances - check the press for details of their latest productions.

MAISON DESCARTES Vijzelgracht 2a.
Tram 16, 24, 25. •f10-f20.
Film shows and theatrical performances organized by the French Consulate to promote French culture and Dutch classics.

DE BRAKKE GROND Nes 45.
Tram 4, 9, 16, 24, 25.
Theatre which occasionally presents a variety of dramatic performances in English.

The Jordaan

APPROX. 2 hr.

Start at the Westerkerk, which is worth visiting not least for the view from the top of its impressive tower (see **CHURCHES**, **Religious Services**). Rembrandt (see **A-Z**) is supposed to be buried here, but the only evidence of this is a memorial plaque. The Gay Monument stands outside on the Westermarkt (see **MONUMENTS**).

The Westerkerk is situated beside the outermost of Amsterdam's girdle of main canals, the Prinsengracht (see **CANALS & RIVERS**), which forms the eastern boundary of the popular and lively district of the Jordaan (see **CITY DISTRICTS**, **A-Z**). Before entering this part of town, turn right and walk along the canal until you come to Anne Frank's House (see **MUSEUMS 1**, **A-Z**). There is often a queue of sightseers waiting to get into this small museum, a must for most visitors to Amsterdam.

Cross the canal by the nearest bridge, turn right and then immediately left, and you are on Egelantiersgracht, a smaller canal taking you into the Jordaan. The narrow streets and attractive houses make this a very pleasant area for a stroll, and there are numerous cafés and small shops to enjoy.

The more interesting buildings on Egelantiersgracht are on the odd-numbered side of the street. The facades of the 'Three Houses' at Nos. 61-65 are embellished with wild animals. The former Beguine convent of St Andrieshofje, which has an accessible courtyard, stands further along at No. 107. Retrace your steps and cross the canal by the Hilletjes Bridge before continuing along the even-numbered side to Eerste Egelantiersdwarsstraat on your left. Standing on the corner is the Café 'T Smalle, a distillery founded in 1780 which is famous for its juniper liqueur.

Turn right along Egelantiersstraat, the first street you come to, and stop to admire the 17thC gable at No. 52, which depicts a hand writing a letter. Next door is the entrance to the Claes Claershofje (or Ansloshofje), founded in 1626 and the second Beguine convent of the tour. It was originally the residence of Claes Claersz Anslo, a cloth merchant. Nowadays it provides accommodation for art students. Inside the courtyard there is another exit to the left which takes you back onto Eerste Egelantiersdwarsstraat. Turn right and you soon come to Tuinstraat. Turn left to reach another Beguine convent, the

Westerkerk

'T Curiosa Winkeltje, Jordaan

Regenboogsliefdehofje at Nos. 100-102. It is closed to the public, but some bolder visitors do wander inside for a look around.

Next, turn right at Tweede Tuindwarsstraat and go straight ahead across the Westerstraat to Tichelstraat. There are some interesting gables and facades at Nos. 53 and 33. Turn right into Karthuizersstraat and you will see the Huiszittenweduwenhof (Courtyard of Widows) on your right. It was built in 1650 and is well preserved.

Continue along Karthuizersstraat and Lindenstraat until you reach the Noorderkerk (see **CHURCHES**), Noordermarkt and Prinsengracht.

The Heart of the City

APPROX. 1 hr

Opposite Centraal Station (see **OFFICIAL BUILDINGS**) you will see
Damrak, the main thoroughfare leading to Dam Square (see **SQUARES**,
A-Z). Follow it, and on the way take a look at the facade of the office
building on the right at Nos. 28-30 - you will see four baboons and 22
owls staring down at you. Opposite is the stock exchange building,
Beurs, which dates from 1903 (see **OFFICIAL BUILDINGS**, **Architecture**).
It still looks modern so it is easy to see why it originally aroused such
controversy. In front is the Beursplein, a favourite with roller skaters,
and at the other end of the square, De Bijenkorf, the large department
store (see **SHOPPING 1**). On the pavement opposite stands the statue of a
man with a newspaper under his arm, which was donated to the city by
the local newspaper *Financiaal Dagblad*.
Continue along the Damrak until you reach Dam Square. To your left is
the National Monument inside of which are enclosed 12 urns of soil,
one from each of the country's provinces and one from the former
colony of Indonesia (see **MONUMENTS**). Facing the monument is the
Royal Palace (see **OFFICIAL BUILDINGS, MUSEUMS 1, A-Z**) and next to it
the Nieuwe Kerk (see **CHURCHES**, **Festivals and Events**). On either side
of the church at Gravenstraat 125 are what appear to be Amsterdam's
smallest shops. Take the Mozes en Aaronstraat between the church and
the palace and you come out on Nieuwezijds Voorburgwal in front of
the main Post Office with its pear-shaped towers (see **OFFICIAL BUILD-
INGS, A-Z**). The curious Spaarpottenmuseum stands on the other side of
Raadhuisstraat (see **MUSEUMS 4**). Don't cross the street, instead turn left
round the back of the palace and return to Dam Square via Paleisstraat.
The first street on the right is Kalverstraat, a pedestrian precinct
crammed with a variety of shops. Look out for the porch at No. 92. It
dates from 1592 and is the entrance to a former orphanage which is
now the Amsterdams Historisch Museum (see **MUSEUMS 2**). Continue
along Kalverstraat, turn right at the first main intersection and you are
on Spui (see **SQUARES**). Scan the wall on your right for the small door at
No. 14 which is the entrance to the Begijnhof (see **MONUMENTS, A-Z**).
Explore the Engelse Kerk and the Catholic Church (see **CHURCHES**,
Religious Services) before taking a look at the oldest house in the city
at No. 34 - its wooden gable dates from about 1475.

Spui to Museumplein

APPROX. 1 hr.

Begin your walk with a visit to the Begijnhof (see **MONUMENTS**, **WALK 2**, **A-Z**) off Spui (see **SQUARES**) before going into the square for a look at Het Lieverdje - Amsterdam's 'Little Darling' (see **MONUMENTS**). Head for the Café Hoppe (see **CAFÉS**, **Brown Cafés**), passing the Athenaeum Bookshop (see **SHOPPING 2**) on your right. Cross the Spuistraat and take the Heisteeg, a narrow passage, over the Singel (see **CANALS & RIVERS**, **Canals**). Carry straight on to Wilde Heisteeg. No. 4 has a sign outside depicting a yawning man and used to be an apothecary's shop. When you reach the bridge over the Herengracht (see **CANALS & RIVERS**, **Canals**) stop to admire the view of the canal and the various types of gable (see **A-Z**) on the houses lining it. Turn left after the bridge and look out for the Bijbels Museum at No. 366 (see **MUSEUMS 2**).

No. 380, built in the 19thC for a rich tobacco planter, is decorated with sculptures of double-headed angels. Nos. 390-392 have neck gables depicting a man and a woman in 17thC costume. Continue along the Herengracht past the Leidsegracht and Leidsestraat until you come to the famous Golden Bend where the most expensive and magnificent houses in Amsterdam were built in the 17thC. Note the double stairways and the splendid entrances.

Next turn right and follow the Nieuwe Spiegelstraat, which contains many antique shops. The Rijksmuseum is ahead of you at the far end of the street (see **MUSEUMS 1**, **A-Z**). Walk towards it, passing the Kerkstraat (which is beginning to rival Nieuwe Spiegelstraat for antique dealers) and turn left into Eerste Weteringdwarsstraat where there is an old secret Beguine convent at Nos. 19-35. Push open the gate of the Grilshofje (as it is called) and enter through the porch, respecting the quiet of the courtyard. Notice the unique Louis XVI clock.

Back on Eerste Weteringdwarsstraat continue on to the Vijzelgracht which runs south from the Muntplein (see **SQUARES**) to the Singelgracht (not to be confused with the Singel). Turn right into the Vijzelgracht, walk to the bridge, and the Rijksmuseum is the immense building on your right. Beyond it is the Museumplein district (see **CITY DISTRICTS**), where you will find the renowned Vincent Van Gogh and Stedelijk museums (see **MUSEUMS 1**, **A-Z**) and the equally famous Concertgebouw (see **OFFICIAL BUILDINGS**, **THEATRE & CINEMA 1**, **A-Z**).

The Red Light District

APPROX. 1:30 hr

From Centraal Station (see **OFFICIAL BUILDINGS**) turn left along Prins Hendrikkade towards the Oosterdok and you see the St Nicolaaskerk (see **CHURCHES**, **Religious Services**). A little further on, at the head of the Geldersekade, is the Schreierstoren (see **MONUMENTS, A-Z**), the unofficial entrance to Amsterdam's notorious Red Light District (see **CITY DISTRICTS, A-Z**). Walk along the right-hand side of the Geldersekade until you reach Nieuwmarkt (see **Markets**). Drug pushers are a common sight here, so you may not wish to linger too long. Turn sharp right along the Zeedijk for a few metres, and then go left along Molensteeg. This takes you across the canals to the imposing Oude Kerk, Amsterdam's oldest and largest church (see **CHURCHES**, **Religious Services**).

The tiny Wijde Kerksteeg behind the church leads to Warmoesstraat, which was once the most desirable address in the city, but is now decidedly seedy. There is an attractive tea and coffee shop at No. 66. The facade of the house opposite, which was once the residence of a cloth merchant, is embellished with a carved ox head. Go north along Warmoesstraat in the direction of Centraal Station and take the second turning on the right into Lange Niezel. The Amstelkring Museum stands on the left where the street rejoins Oudezijds Voorburgwal (see **MUSEUMS 2**). Known as *Our Dear Lord in the Attic*, this is one of the most interesting of Amsterdam's small museums.

Cross the canal, head along the Korte Niezel, and turn right along the Oudezijds Achterburgwal into the centre of the Red Light area, where prostitutes sit impassively in the windows advertizing their availability. Two 17thC warehouses stand near the junction with Molensteeg. One of them has a bas-relief of a boat caught in a storm, and a fortress with the inscription 'God is my Castle'. Next to it is the 'Old Sailor', containing maritime souvenirs (there is a model ship above the entrance).

Cross the canal and head south, passing the Waalse Kerk on your left and the Stadhuis (see **OFFICIAL BUILDINGS**) on your right, until you reach the Grimburgwal. To the left is the former Binnengasthuis Hospital, now university buildings. Cross the bridge towards Oudezijds Voorburgwal again and you will see the 'House of Three Canals'. Ahead is Langebrugsteeg, leading to the busy thoroughfare of Rokin.

The Main Canals

APPROX. 4 hr

Start at the northern end of Singel (see CANALS & RIVERS, **Canals**), where you will see the Ronde Lutherse Kerk (see CHURCHES) on your left. The best view is from the other side of the canal. Very near the church, at Singel 7, there is a remarkably narrow house which is a popular subject for holiday snaps. Continue south along the canal as far as Blauburgwal and then turn right, crossing the Herengracht (see CANALS & RIVERS) and Keizersgracht (see CANALS & RIVERS) to reach the Prinsengracht (see CANALS & RIVERS). Turn left along the canal and stop to admire the 18thC courtyard at No. 159. Anne Frank's House (see MUSEUMS 1, A-Z) and the Westerkerk (see CHURCHES, **Religious Services**) are further along on the same side of the street. After the busy Raadhuisstraat, turn left at Reestraat to reach Keizersgracht once more. Turn right and enjoy the views of the fine buildings on both sides of the canal - especially of the Shaffy Theatre (see THEATRE & CINEMA 2). The side streets along here contain interesting little shops (see SHOPPING 4). Take Huidenstraat on the left to reach Herengracht at the point where the famous Golden Bend begins. The Bijbels Museum (see MUSEUMS 2) is on your right, and the stretch of canal from here to Vijzelstraat is lined with many opulent mansions. Next on the right after Vijzelgracht is Reguliersgracht (see CANALS & RIVERS), with its famous view of seven canal bridges in a row. Head in the opposite direction, along the garish Thorbeckeplein, and turn left after Rembrandtsplein (see SQUARES, A-Z) into Reguliersbree-straat, home of the famous Tuschinski Cinema (see MONUMENTS, THE-ATRE & CINEMA 1). This street leads to the Muntplein (see SQUARES) at the southern end of Singel. The Drijvende Bloemenmarkt (see A-Z) on the left bank creates a bustling, colourful scene.

Aalsmeer: 16 km from Amsterdam. Pop: 21,000.
A town near Schiphol (see **Airport**) notable for the Bloemenveiling (Flower Auction) held all year round in the enormous auction hall at Legmeerdijk 313 (0730-1100 Mon.-Fri.). A visitors' gallery gives a splendid view of the trading area, with its spectacular and colourful arrays of flowers. See **EXCURSION 3**.

Accidents and Breakdowns: If you are involved in a motoring accident follow the normal procedure of exchanging names, addresses and insurance details with the other party, while saying nothing that could be considered an admission of liability. Telephone the police on 22 22 22 if the accident is serious, or medical services on 555 55 55 if there are casualties.
In the event of a breakdown, move your car off the road (if possible) and place a hazard warning triangle an adequate distance behind the vehicle. AA and RAC members may use the services of their Dutch equivalent, the Dutch Automobile Association Emergency Service (ANWB), tel: (020) 26 82 51. Temporary membership costs very little. See **Driving**.

Accommodation: Amsterdam is well provided with hotels of all categories, from the most basic to the most luxurious. A double room can cost as little as f60 or as much as f475 per night. As you would expect, comfort and facilities provided are reflected in the price, so it is advisable to look at the room before registering, especially in cheaper hotels. The VVV (see **Tourist Information**) will book accommodation for a fee of f3,50, but postal requests for this service are not accepted. See **Camping and Caravanning**, **Youth Hostels**.

Airport: Schiphol, 15 km from Amsterdam on the A 10 and A 9 motorways, is one of the world's most popular airports, as numerous consumer surveys prove. It handles flights to and from all the major international destinations.

Alkmaar: 35 km from Amsterdam. Pop: 84,000.
A well-preserved town, established by the 13thC, with much to interest

the visitor. The St Laurenskerk (1470-1516), also called the Grote Kerk, is Gothic in style, and includes a 17thC organ and pulpit, and a vault painting by Cornelis Buys. The Stedelijk Museum at Doelenstraat 3 has exhibits on town history and paintings by many of the lesser lights of the Golden Age. The tower of the Waag (public weighing-house) in the main square features clockwork jousting knights. A great attraction is the Kaasmarkt (Cheese Market) held in the Waagplein every Friday morning during the summer months. The pleasant coastal resorts of Egmond aan Zee and Bergen aan Zee are to be found just outside Alkmaar. See **EXCURSION 2**.

Alphen aan de Rijn: 36 km from Amsterdam. Pop: 55,000.
The main attraction of this town is the Avifauna Bird Sanctuary, which contains nearly 300 species of birds, many of them exotic, and keeps them in conditions sympathetic to their accustomed habitats in the wild. It is open all year round, until 2100 during the summer months and 1800 in winter.

Amersfoort: 41 km from Amsterdam. Pop: 87,000.
A pleasant town with many canals, squares and quaint little streets. The St Joriskerk dates mainly from the 15th and 16thC, but the tower has stonework from the mid-13thC. The Koppelpoort, an ancient water-gate over the River Eem, was restored in the late 19thC by P. J. H. Cuypers (see **Architecture**). Historic and prehistoric artefacts from Amersfoort and the nearby city of Utrecht (see **A-Z**) can be seen in the Museum Flehite at Westsingel 50.

Architecture: Although Amsterdam's Gothic remains suggest that the buildings of earlier times were impressive, it was the architecture of Hendrick de Keyser, Jacob van Campen and Philips Vingboons (who were responsible for introducing the Renaissance styles in the 17thC) which really established the city as a centre of excellence in this field. Examples of their work include the Munttoren (see **MONUMENTS**, **A-Z**), the Royal Palace (see **OFFICIAL BUILDINGS**, **MUSEUMS 1**, **WALK 2**, **A-Z**) and many churches, including the Westerkerk, the Noorderkerk and the Zuiderkerk (see **CHURCHES**).

The next great advance was the neo-Gothic style of P. J. H. Cuypers (see **MUSEUMS 1**, **OFFICIAL BUILDINGS**, **Rijksmuseum**) in the late 19thC, which was superseded by the highly influential Hendrik P. Berlage, who ushered in a new era of architecture with his innovative design for the Beurs (see **OFFICIAL BUILDINGS**, **WALK 2**).

A group inspired by Berlage, and known as the Amsterdam School, produced some outstanding housing developments in a frantic burst of creativity around the 1920s. To the fore of the group were Michael de Klerk and P. L. Kramer.

Succeeding movements, such as the group known as De Stijl, reacted against the elaborate style of the Amsterdam School. An outstanding example of their more functional approach to design is Gerrit Rietveld's Van Gogh Museum (see **MUSEUMS 1**, **A-Z**).

Development continues today, and there is much to admire in the blending of new buildings with old in many parts of Amsterdam, such as the Jordaan (see **CITY DISTRICTS**, **WALK 1**, **A-Z**).

Babysitters: Your hotel will probably be able to arrange a babysitter for you. Rates are approx. f4 per hr before 2400, f5 per hr 2400-0300, and f10 per hr after 0300. Also tel: 23 17 08 between 1730 and 1900 for the Student Babysitting Service.

A-Z

BAN

Banks: They offer all the usual facilities. Centraal Station has a branch of the GWK (Grenwisselkantoor) which is open 0700-2245 daily. There are also many exchange kiosks on the main streets in the city centre which are open conveniently long hours, but offer less favourable terms. See **Opening Times**.

Begijnhof: Situated off Spui (see SQUARES), the Begijnhof is a quiet courtyard in a former convent for Beguine nuns. A secret chapel (see **Religious Services**) was built following the Reformation, and the main church, the Engelse Kerk (see CHURCHES, **Religious Services**), was taken over by Scottish Presbyterians. Both can be visited, as can one of Amsterdam's oldest houses - a wooden structure originally built in the late 15thC. However, the main attraction of the Begijnhof may well be the peace and quiet of this secluded area lying right in the heart of the city. See MONUMENTS, WALK 2 & 3.

Best Buys: Flowers can vary in price according to the season, but they are always remarkably cheap. House plants are also very good value. The Flower Market (see **Drijvende Bloemenmarkt**) offers a wide choice (see **Tulips**). You are allowed to bring up to two kilos of bulbs or tubers, five plants or cuttings, five packets of seeds and one small bunch of flowers into Britain. Chinaware is also a good buy. There is a great deal of imitation Delft china around so be careful. The real thing is more expensive, but still cheaper than outside the Netherlands (see **Delft**). Amsterdam is also famous for diamonds (see **A-Z**), which are less expensive here than just about anywhere else in the world. See SHOPPING, **Souvenirs**.

Bicycle Hire: Hire shops are plentiful, especially near the railway stations. The daily rate is approx. f7, the weekly rate approx. f28. A deposit of f100-f200 is usually required. You will lose this deposit if the bike is stolen - theft is very common, so beware. See **Bicycles**.

Bicycles: An ideal way to see Amsterdam, because of the compactness of the city and the excellent facilities provided for cyclists. A charming feature of the city is the sight of swarms of Amsterdammers fearlessly weaving in and out of the busy traffic. Inexperienced riders will find that the many cycle lanes make life easier. The entire country is geared to the bike, and all the trains will accommodate them if you want to go further afield. You must have reflectors on your wheels and keep in single file at all times (even in cycle lanes). See **Bicycle Hire**.

Boat Hire: Sailing boats, complete with skipper, can be hired from De Ruijterkade behind Centraal Station (see **OFFICIAL BUILDINGS**), and elsewhere, at a cost of approx. f75 per hr. A four-person motorboat costs about f37,50 per hr. The small towns along the coast of the Markermeer and IJsselmeer (see **EXCURSION 1, A-Z**) provide excellent mooring facilities. All boats for hire are insured, but a hefty deposit will be required.

Brown Cafés: So called because of their dark wooden furnishings and nicotine-stained walls. Many of these traditional cafés are centuries old. Although sparsely decorated, they provide a friendly and relaxed atmosphere, and are ideal places for a coffee or a quiet drink during the day, or a chat with locals during the evening. Most provide basic snacks, if not full meals. You will find a brown café on virtually every corner in the Jordaan (see **CITY DISTRICTS, WALK 1, A-Z**), although some of these tend to be rather artificial versions of the real thing, which is typified by the famous Café Hoppe. See **CAFÉS**.

Budget:

Food and Drink	Breakfast f10-f20.
	Lunch f20-f30.
	Dinner f50-f100.
	Sandwiches f3,50-f6,50.
	Beer f2-f3.
	Spirit and mixer f6.
	Soft drink f2-f3.
Tobacco	20 Cigarettes f3,75.
	10 Cigars f8-f50 plus.
	50 g hand-rolling tobacco f4.
Entertainment	Cinema f6-f12.
	Theatre f10-f50.
Things to see	Museums f1-f7; or f30 for Museumcards valid for one year giving access to all state museums - available from the VVV (see **Tourist Information**).
	Churches f1-f2, but mostly free.
Rentals	Bicycle f8-f10 per day (f100-f200 deposit).
	Car f60-f120 per day.
	Pedalo f18,50-f27,50per hr.
Transport	Bus and Tram Ticket f8,65 (day), f25 (week).
	Canal Tour f8 (one hr).
	Taxi f50 (Schiphol Airport to Dam Square).

Buses: A number of bus companies provide services to all parts of the city. They operate on the *strippenkaart* fare system (see **Transport**), although daily or weekly tickets, which can be purchased from the VVV (see **Tourist Information**), are more economical if you intend to use public transport regularly. External coach routes also link Amsterdam to other parts of the Netherlands and beyond. See **Tours and Excursions**.

Cameras and Photography: Flash photography is not permitted in some museums and churches - enquire beforehand.
There are shops catering for all photographic requirements, but film is expensive so bring a good supply with you.

Camping and Caravanning: Amsterdam has six main camping sites of a high standard. Advance booking is usually advisable. They charge approx. f3,50 to f10 per night per person (car included). Tent hire is from as little as f1. See **PARKS**.

Canal Bike Hire: A four-person canal bike (pedalo) costs approx. f27,50 per hour, a two-person bike f18,50 per hour. You can hire them at the Singelgracht, near Leidseplein, and the Prinsengracht, at Westermarkt.

Canals: Amsterdam abounds in waterways, but the only natural one is the Amstel River. The town began to grow after this was dammed in the 13thC, and a ring of canals (*grachtengordel*) was built as the city expanded. From the centre outwards, these are the Singel, the Herengracht, the Keizersgracht and the Prinsengracht. They are lined by fine merchants' houses and large warehouses, providing many attractive views. The Brouwersgracht, which runs along the north end of the main canals, and other minor canals running through the Red Light District (see **CITY DISTRICTS**, **WALK 4**, **A-Z**), the old town and the dockland areas east of the city centre, are especially picturesque. Nowadays there is little commercial traffic on the canals, but you will often see boatloads of sightseers passing along them. For many people this is one of the most fascinating ways to see the city (and places of interest along the way are pointed out by the guides). See **CANALS & RIVERS**, **CHILDREN**, **WALK 5**, **Tours and Excursions**.

Car Hire: All the major international companies are represented in the Netherlands and can be found at Schiphol (see **Airport**). Few firms have offices in the centre of Amsterdam, but those which do are listed in the Yellow Pages under *Autoverhuur*. Hiring a car is only really worthwhile for touring outside the city. Rates are approx. f60-f120 per day. See **Driving**.

Chemists: Follow normal opening hours Mon.-Fri. and a rota system for evenings and weekends. Tel: 13 28 55 for the address of the nearest open pharmacy. See **Opening Times**.

Children: Youngsters are well catered for in the Netherlands. There is no shortage of museums, theatres and parks providing facilities and entertainment for their enjoyment. Families are welcome in most cafés, bars and restaurants, but if in doubt check beforehand. See **CHILDREN**, **Babysitters**.

Cigarettes and Tobacco: Cigarettes are sold in packets of 20 or 25 in many hotels and restaurants as well as shops and from vending machines. The familiar international brands are all available, but are slightly more expensive than local brands, which cost around f3,50. Holland is famous for its cigars, and tobacconists provide a huge selection ranging from the very cheap to the very expensive. Hand-rolling tobacco and pipe tobacco are also good value. See **SHOPPING 4**. The no-smoking policy in Amsterdam is not yet as aggressive as in many other cities, but you should observe the rules in public places such as restaurants.

Climate: The weather in the Netherlands is typical of north-western European countries - generally mild, with few extremes either in winter or summer, but unpredictable at all times. For example, visitors should be prepared for sudden showers, even in the summertime. July and August are normally the warmest months (average temperature approx. 20°C), but spring is usually drier than summer.

Concertgebouw: This world-famous concert hall, located on the Museumplein (see **CITY DISTRICTS**, **SQUARES**) was completed in 1888 to a design by A. L. van Gendt. The resident orchestra built up its reputation under the direction of Willem Kes and Willem Mengelberg over the ensuing decades, and that reputation remains high today. The splendid acoustics in the hall make it a treat for music lovers. Free concerts are held at 1230 on Wednesdays throughout the year, and the summertime evening concerts are not expensive. Check the press for details of performances during the season (which runs from September to March) and during the Holland Festival (see **Festivals and Events**). The hall serves as a venue for rock as well as classical concerts. See **OFFICIAL BUILDINGS**, **THEATRE & CINEMA 1**, **WALK 3**.

Consulates:
United Kingdom - Koningslaan 44, Amsterdam. Tel: 76 43 43.
Republic of Ireland - Willemskade 23, Rotterdam. Tel: (010) 14 33 22.
United States - Museumplein 19, Amsterdam. Tel: 79 03 21/71 70 30.
Canada - Sophialaan 7, The Hague. Tel: (070) 61 41 11.
Australia - Koninginnegracht 23, The Hague. Tel: (070) 63 09 83.
New Zealand - Mauritskade 25, The Hague. Tel: (070) 46 93 24.

Conversion Charts:

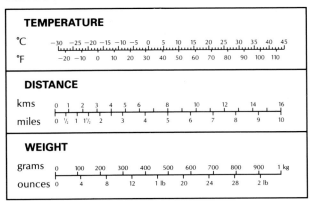

Credit Cards: Most larger stores, restaurants and hotels accept all the major credit cards.

Crime and Theft: Amsterdam is a reasonably safe city, but there are still risks. Beware of pickpockets at all times and keep an eye on your bike as theft is very common. Keep to busy well-lit streets at night, or travel by taxi. The Red Light District (see **CITY DISTRICTS**, **WALK 4**, **A-Z**) actually has a more intimidating air during daylight hours as drug addicts and pushers are a common sight but, by and large, they will not bother you if you ignore them. Should you run into trouble you will find the Police Headquarters at Elandsgracht 117 (tel: 559 91 11), and there are police services for overseas visitors at Waterlooplein 9, tel: 559 33 95 (0900-1500 Mon.-Wed. & Fri.). See **Emergencies**.

Currency: The guilder is the national monetary unit of the Netherlands (abbreviated as Dfl, Fl, or f). There are 100 cents (ct) to the guilder. Coins in circulation are worth 5ct, 10ct, 25ct, f1, f2,50 and f5. Notes are in denominations of f5, f10, f25, f50, f100 and f1000.

Customs:

Duty Paid Into:	Cigarettes	or	Cigars	or	Tobacco	Spirits	Wine
E.E.C.	300		75		400 g	1.5 *l*	5 *l*
U.K.	300		75		400 g	1.5 *l*	5 *l*

Dam Square: Known by the locals simply as Dam. It was on this site that the Amstel River (see **CANALS & RIVERS**) was dammed in the 13thC, starting the growth of the city (see **History**). The Stadhuis, or Town Hall, was built on the square and later converted to the Royal Palace (see **MUSEUMS 1**, **OFFICIAL BUILDINGS**, **A-Z**). Next door is the Nieuwe Kerk, which serves as the royal chapel and is the location for state occasions such as the 1980 coronation of Queen Beatrix (see **CHURCHES**). Opposite is the National Monument (see **MONUMENTS**). Dam is the real heart of the city, and a good starting point for visiting the main shopping streets (see **CITY DISTRICTS**), the main canals (see **CANALS & RIVERS**), and the old town (see **CITY DISTRICTS**, **WALK 4**, **Red Light District**). Many tram routes pass through the square, which is often vibrant with street entertainment. See **WALK 2**.

Delft: 60 km from Amsterdam. Pop: 86,000.
This town near The Hague (see **A-Z**) has many attractions, not least of which is the famous pottery which bears its name (see **Best Buys**). Two Gothic churches, the Nieuwe Kerk and the Oude Kerk, stand near one another in the town centre; and the main museums are the Prinsenhof and the Huis Lambert van Meerten. The former is notable as the place where William the Silent, Prince of Orange, was assassinated in 1584. Historical artefacts are exhibited here. The Huis Lambert van Meerten has impressive displays of Delftware. The pottery can also be admired (and bought) at numerous factory showrooms and shops. The prettiness of Delft makes it a pleasant place for a leisurely stroll. Some of its street scenes were painted by Vermeer (see **A-Z**), the town's most famous son, and the atmosphere he captured has certainly survived.

Dentists: 24-hr information on dental care is available from the Central Medical Service. See **Emergencies**.

Diamonds: Amsterdam has been associated with diamonds since the 16thC, when Jewish immigrants first introduced the trade to the city. The discovery of diamonds in South Africa in the 1860s heralded a time of expansion for the industry, with Amsterdam very much to the fore. The biggest diamond ever discovered, the Cullinan, was cut here (as was the famous Koh-i-Noor) and the city remains one of the world's foremost centres for this glamorous trade. Guided tours of the factories enable you to admire the skills of the craftsmen as they cut and polish the precious stones. There are also numerous diamond shops in the city centre should you wish to buy or just window-shop. See **Best Buys**.

Dikes: Without its vast programme of land reclamation, the Netherlands as we know it would not exist. About half of its 13 million inhabitants live on land won back from the sea by means of the extensive system of dikes. Basically, the process involves walling off an area and draining it with pumps. The water is removed to the canals, which carry it eventually to the sea, and selected crops of reeds and rapeseed are sown to assist in the drying and reconditioning of the soil. The apparent simplicity of this system belies the reality of the continual struggle to keep the sea at bay. Pumping stations must operate constantly to prevent flooding, and freak weather conditions can have disastrous effects. For the visitor, the diked Dutch countryside provides an opportunity for enjoying a vast flat landscape, often bathed in colour at flower-gathering time, which is ideal for the cyclist. Surprisingly large vessels make their way along the canals above the level of the road - impressive proof of the engineering achievements of the dike builders.

Disabled: Facilities for the disabled are fairly good throughout the Netherlands, although the old buildings and narrow streets obviously create difficulties. The Netherlands Board of Tourism, 25-28 Buckingham Gate, London SW1E 6LD, can provide a list of hotels, restaurants and places of interest with suitable facilities.

Doctors: 24-hr information on medical care is available from the Central Medical Service. See **Emergencies**.

Drijvende Bloemenmarkt (Floating Flower Market):
Located on the Singel (see CANALS & RIVERS, **Canals**) between Muntplein (see SQUARES) and Koningsplein, and open 0900-1600 Mon.-Sat. A vast range of inexpensive bulbs, cuttings, flowers and pot plants is sold from stalls floating on the canal, making the market one of the city's most colourful sights. See WALK 5, **Best Buys**.

Drinks: The most popular alcoholic drink in Holland is beer, served German-style with a large frothy head. But for a taste of traditional Dutch spirits try a glass of *jenever* (see **Tasting Houses**), a drink which gave its name to gin, but is weaker and tastes slightly different to the British version. Both young and old varieties are available, as are blackcurrant (*bessenjenever*) and lemon (*citroenjenever*) flavours, as well as *bittertje,* the Dutch version of pink gin. There is also the famous eggy, yellow *advocaat*, which is the main constituent of a snowball cocktail. Imported wines and liqueurs tend to be more expensive. There are no licensing restrictions in Amsterdam, so cafés and bars set their own opening times.
The popular non-alcoholic drinks include coffee (usually excellent), tea

(to a lesser extent) and the usual range of soft and fizzy drinks, as well as fruit juices.

Driving: If you are taking your car to the Netherlands you will need a valid national driving licence, your car registration papers and a national identity sign on the vehicle. Hiring a car just for getting about the city is not advisable due to traffic congestion and parking difficulties (see **Parking**). Remember to drive on the right and overtake on the left. Give way to trams, pedestrians at crossings and traffic from the right. Observe the speed restrictions (generally 50 kph in built-up areas, 80 kph on main roads, 100 kph on motorways). Be particularly vigilant in looking out for cyclists. The wearing of seat belts is compulsory. See **Accidents and Breakdowns**, **Car Hire**.

Drugs: Contrary to many people's expectations, drugs are not legal in Amsterdam. In practice, however, the authorities generally turn a blind eye to the sale, possession and consumption of small amounts of cannabis. It is readily obtainable in the many cafés which display the sign of a cannabis plant in the window. Hard drugs such as cocaine and heroin are quite another matter, and if you are caught in possession of these you could face a prison sentence. It is not uncommon to see addicts and dealers on the streets. Because of Amsterdam's reputation as a drugs centre customs officials are extremely vigilant, so it is foolish to try to get the better of them. The Drugs Advice Centre is situated at Keizersgracht 812 (1300-1500 Mon.-Fri.). See **Emergencies**.

Edam: 22 km from Amsterdam. Pop: 24,000.
This exceptionally pretty coastal town close to Volendam (see **A-Z**) on the Markermeer (see **A-Z**) is famous for giving its name to the round cheese, which is actually not as popular in the Netherlands as Gouda. The Kaasmarkt (Cheese Market) is one of its main attractions, as is the local museum at Damplein 8. Explore the town's canals and streets, which are lined with picturesque houses. See **EXCURSION 1**.

Electricity: 220 volts. Two-pin plugs are used and adapters can be purchased in electrical shops in Britain and the Netherlands.

Emergencies:

Police - Tel: 22 22 22.
Fire Brigade - Tel: 21 21 21.
Accidents and Medical Care - Tel: 555 55 55.
Central Medical Service - Tel: 64 21 11.
Social Services - Tel: 16 16 66.
Drugs Help Line - Tel: 94 84 60.

Enkhuizen: 62 km from Amsterdam. Pop: 16,000.

A harbour town on the IJsselmeer (see **A-Z**) with some churches and
other buildings of interest, but whose main attraction is the remarkable
Zuider Zee Museum, consisting of the Binnenmuseum (indoor) and the
Buitenmuseum (outdoor). The former is housed in large converted
warehouses surrounding a central courtyard, and exhibits maritime
artefacts and furniture relating to the history of the area (Apr.-Oct.
1000-1700 Mon.-Sat., 1200-1700 Sun.). The Buitenmuseum can only
be reached by ferry from the town's main jetty (Apr.-Oct. 1000-1700).
Here you can wander around reconstructions of local fishing villages.
Shops sell traditional handicrafts as well as mass-produced souvenirs,
and there are interesting demonstrations of crafts such as boat building.
See **EXCURSION 1**.

Festivals and Events:

February: The Carnival, starting with a parade from the Oosterdok to
Rembrandtsplein (see **SQUARES**, **A-Z**) - fancy dress, dancing, lots of beer
and non-stop music in the streets.
March: The Concertgebouw Orchestra's Easter programme (see **OFFICIAL
BUILDINGS, THEATRE & CINEMA 1**, **WALK 3**, **A-Z**); Nieuwe Kerk Antique Fair
(see **CHURCHES**).
April: Electrische Museumtramlijn - rides from Karperweg 44 to the
Amsterdamse Bos (see **PARKS**) on vintage trams (until Oct.);
30th: Queen's Day - public holiday with street musicians, stalls, events.
May: Kunst RAI - art fair at the exhibition hall (see **OFFICIAL BUILDINGS**);
15th: Antiques Market on Beursplein (until Sept.).
June: Holland Festival - Art Exhibitions, Dance, Music and Theatre;
Vondelpark Festival (see **PARKS**, **A-Z**) - open-air events, an adjunct to the

Holland Festival; 25th: Street festival, the Dome Quarter.
July-August: Summer programmes in many theatres.
August: Uitmarkt - start of the cultural season.
September: Jordaan Festival (see **CITY DISTRICTS**, **WALK 1**, **A-Z**);
First Saturday: Flower Parade from Aalsmeer (see **A-Z**) to Amsterdam.
October: Autumn Opening and Art Exhibition in the Royal Palace (see
MUSEUMS 1, **OFFICIAL BUILDINGS**, **WALK 2**, **A-Z**).
November: 25th St Nicolaas Parade.

Flea Market: Temporarily situated on Valkenburgerstraat near the Waterlooplein (see **SQUARES**), but due to return to the square itself. Bargains are to be found amongst the stalls selling second-hand clothes, books, antiques and household goods, but haggling is not the done thing (1000-1600 Mon.-Sat.).

Food: Traditional Dutch food is fairly plain and filling, and you will not go hungry even on a restricted budget. Breakfast consists of eggs, cheese, various cold meats, and bread rolls and jam. Many kinds of snacks are sold on the streets, the speciality being seafood like herring (see **Maatjes**), mackerel and eel. A wide variety of *broodjes* (filled bread rolls) are also available. An *uitsmijter,* consisting of bread, fried eggs, and a topping of ham or cheese, makes for an inexpensive meal. The most favoured cheeses are Edam and Gouda. Other staple dishes include thick soups, cold meats, sausages and waffles. A traditional dinner consists of typical north-western European fare such as stews or grills; while a wide variety of ethnic restaurants provide a selection of more exotic dishes. See **RESTAURANTS**, **Restaurants**.

Frank, Anne (1929-1945): Born into a Jewish family in Frankfurt, Anne Frank and her relations fled from the Nazis in 1933 and settled in Amsterdam. The Nazi occupation of 1942 spelt further danger, and the family took refuge in a secret back room at Prinsengracht 236 (see **MUSEUMS 1**) where Anne wrote her famous diary which has become such an important testimony to the suffering of the Jews. The little group was betrayed to the Germans in 1944 and Anne died in Belsen concentration camp the following year. The house has been preserved just as it was in her time, and is undeniably a most moving place to visit. Exhibitions record the unfortunate continuation of racist and anti-Semitic thought in many quarters today.

Gables: Because canal houses were at one time taxed according to the widths of their facades, many of even the grandest houses were very narrow in construction. For a rich merchant, one way of compensating for this lack of frontage was to adorn the roof with an impressive gable to advertize his status. A walk along the canals will reveal the

astonishing variety of shapes and styles employed: neck, column, bell, step and spout, to name but a few. Sculpted figures often illustrate the trade of the original occupant. See **Houses**.

Gambling: The Casino Amsterdam at the Hilton Hotel, Apollolaan 138 (1400-0300, day ticket f7,50) features roulette, blackjack and gaming machines. Smart attire is necessary. Amusement arcades are also to be found in the main tourist areas such as Damrak, Rembrandtsplein, Muntplein and Leidseplein (see SQUARES, A-Z).

Gouda: 50 km from Amsterdam. Pop: 60,000.
World-famous for its cheese, which the Dutch prefer to Edam cheese. The Cheese Market is held in the market square every Thursday from June to August (0900-1200). The nearby Gothic Stadhuis is supposed to be the oldest town hall in the Netherlands, and the St Janskerk boasts an impressive array of stained-glass windows, many predating the fire of 1552 which destroyed much of the church. The windows commissioned to replace those lost depict many of the outstanding figures of the mid-16thC.

Haarlem: 20 km from Amsterdam. Pop: 152,000.
Two of the major influences forming Haarlem's distinctive character are the tulip trade (see **A-Z**), and its nearby beach resort (see **Zandvoort**). The painter Franz Hals, who spent the greater part of his life here, has a museum named after him (converted from a hospice designed by another notable Haarlemmer, the architect Lieven de Key), which is dedicated to his life and work. The Teylers Museum at Spaarne 16 was founded in 1778, making it the oldest existing museum in the Netherlands. Unfortunately its antiquity is all too apparent, although it does contain some interesting exhibits of scientific instruments and some sketches by Rembrandt (see **A-Z**), Raphael and Michelangelo. Elsewhere, the Grote Kerk and its environs are evocative of the old Holland. Haarlem has the reputation of being a lively nightspot (especially enjoyable after a day on the beach at nearby Zandvoort), and is conveniently located for a trip south to the heart of the tulip country. See EXCURSION 2.

Hague, The: 60 km from Amsterdam. Pop: 445,000.
Known by the Dutch as Den Haag, rather than by its more formal name of 's-Gravenhage, this is an elegant city, as befits a seat of government and a centre of royal and state occasions. The parliament buildings, parts of which have been standing since 13thC, are known as the Binnenhof. Other government buildings and three royal palaces add to the city's grandeur, and there are many fine museums, including the Mauritshuis, which contains the most prestigious art collection in the country. At Zeestraat 65b is the Panorama Mesdag, a massive depiction of the village of Scheveningen, finished by Mesdag in 1881 and one of the very few surviving examples of panoramic painting. The three-dimensional effect is quite extraordinary. The Hague is not all culture and ceremony, however. Its parks are excellent, and the miniature city of Madurodam has great appeal (see **CHILDREN**, **A-Z**).

Hairdressers: There are salons in most of the major hotels. Ask your receptionist to recommend a good local hairdresser if your hotel does not have this facility. Many of the smarter salons are situated in the Old South, in the streets around the Vondelpark (see **PARKS**, **A-Z**) and the Museumplein (see **SQUARES**). A shampoo, cut and blow-dry will cost about f55-f65.

Health: See **Chemists, Dentists, Doctors, Drugs, Emergencies, Hospitals**.

Hilversum: 30 km from Amsterdam. Pop: 88,000.
A pleasant residential city in the heart of the Gooi Forest, mainly notable as the heart of the Netherlands' radio and broadcasting services (see **Television and Radio**). There are many parks designed by W. W. Dudok in this clean attractive town.

History: The city derives its name from the dam built over the Amstel River (see **CANALS & RIVERS**) in the 13thC, on the site of what is now Dam Square (see **SQUARES**, **A-Z**), which led to Amsterdam's growth from a fishing village to a major port. Streets and canals spread out from the dam, gradually and relentlessly pushing back the town's limits until it reached its present proportions. Remains of ancient fortifications which can still be seen today are the Schreierstoren (see **MONUMENTS**,

WALK 4, A-Z) and the Montelbaanstoren on the Oudeschans. The girdle of main canals (see **CANALS & RIVERS**, **A-Z**) that gives the city so much of its character was developed by the 17thC, when the prosperous times known as the Golden Age saw the building of many splendid merchants' houses. Amsterdam's establishment as a centre of Protestantism in these post-Reformation times did not affect the traditional tolerance of its people. Roman Catholics could always find a place to worship (see **CHURCHES**) and Jewish immigrants were readily accommodated. The latter's legacy remains to this day, having survived occupation by the Nazis in the Second World War (see **CHURCHES**, **CITY DISTRICTS**). Modern Amsterdam is a bustling, cosmopolitan centre which provides everything for the visitor, from high culture to low life. The major museums stand comparison with any in the world, beautiful buildings are to be seen everywhere, the complex of canals is picturesque and the city abounds in cultural events and nightlife.

Hospitals: The Netherlands offers a high standard of medical care. The Academisch Medisch Centrum at Meibergdreef 9 is one of the leading hospitals in Amsterdam, and there are casualty clinics offering first-aid services at Oosterparkstraat 179, de Boelelaan 1117, and Oudezijds Voorburgwal 127.

Houses: Built on wooden stakes over the water, many old city houses tilt forward, possibly because of subsidence or possibly because they were specifically constructed this way to avoid erosion of the facades and gables - so the story goes, anyway. The tall, narrow canal houses with their varied facades and gables (see **A-Z**) are a major attraction for the visitor to Amsterdam. Many date from the 17thC, and recent renovation work has assured their survival in trendier parts of the city such as the Jordaan (see **CITY DISTRICTS, WALK 1, A-Z**), which had previously been in decline. Continuing Amsterdam's reputation for excellence in architecture, the Amsterdam School designed many bold and imaginative housing schemes in the 1920s and 30s which still seem fresh and innovative today (see **Architecture**). See **CITY DISTRICTS**.

IJsselmeer: Formerly the Zuider Zee, a tidal sea which for centuries supported a lucrative fishing industry. The construction (1932) of the Afsluitdijk from Den Oever in Noord-Holland to Zurich in Friesland converted the sea to an inland lake, which was renamed the IJsselmeer. Vast tracts of land were diked and drained, thereby reducing the IJsselmeer in size, and further reclamation is proposed for the 1990s. The N 302 dike road, which was opened in the mid-1970s, bisected the lake and the southern part was renamed the Markermeer (see **A-Z**). The lack of a troublesome tide makes the IJsselmeer an ideal boating area, and the old fishing ports on the coast are often visited this way (see **EXCURSION 1**). Even inexperienced sailors should find little difficulty in navigating the lake after some basic training.

Jordaan: A trendy, lively part of Amsterdam to the west of the Prinsengracht (see **CANALS & RIVERS, Canals**) which has undergone a revival in recent years after a period of decline. Once a working-class residential area, it has now become popular with middle-class and artistic members of the community, and bustles with renewed vitality. Its streets and canals are compact and neat, and are all named after plants and flowers. The residents assiduously maintain the area's improved image by planting greenery along the streets and cultivating window-boxes. Every day seems to be marked by the opening of a new shop, and the numerous cafés and craft studios contribute greatly to the agreeable atmosphere which prevails here. See **CITY DISTRICTS**, **WALK 1**.

Keukenhof: An immense, spectacular flower garden in the town of Lisse, 34 km south-west of Amsterdam (0800-1930 Apr.-May). The well-landscaped gardens are crammed with wide-ranging displays of flowers and shrubs. An annual Flower Parade is held in the town at the end of April. See **EXCURSION 3**, **Tulips**.

Laundry and Dry-Cleaning: Launderettes are known as *wasserij* and dry-cleaners as *stomerij*. There are launderettes at Rozengracht 59, Herenstraat 24 and Oude Doelenstraat 12, and one at Warmoesstraat 30 which is open 24 hr.

Leiden: 41 km from Amsterdam. Pop: 104,000.
The town's famous university was established in 1575 by William the Silent, Prince of Orange, as a reward to the inhabitants for their resilience during the year-long siege by the Spanish. It was the first university in the Netherlands, and contributed to Leiden's growth as an academic centre (avowedly Protestant, but on the whole tolerant). It was in Leiden that the non-conformist preacher John Robinson, having been suspended in England in 1604, found the freedom to exercise his Puritan beliefs. He took many followers with him, and in 1620 they became famous as the Pilgrim Fathers when they sailed for America in the *Mayflower* (their leader remaining in Leiden). The Pilgrim Fathers Documents Centre at Boisotkade 2a records the event. There are many other museums, including the Rijksmuseum van Oudheden (archeological findings from ancient Egypt and the Netherlands) and the Stedelijk Museum de Lakenhal, Oude Singel 28-32 (paintings, ceramics and antique furnishings). Another of Leiden's attractions is the Hortus Botanicus at Rapenburg 73, one of the world's first botanical gardens.

Leidseplein: A busy square, situated on the edge of the ring of main canals, and the hub of Amsterdam's nightlife. Amongst the profusion of cinemas, restaurants and cafés, you will find the Stadsschouwburg (see **THEATRE & CINEMA 1**), the American Hotel (see **MONUMENTS**) and the Melkweg complex (see **DISCOS**). An ice-rink is set up in the centre of the square during winter. See **SQUARES**.

Lost and Found:
Police Lost Property Office - Waterlooplein 11, tel: 559 91 11. 1100-1530 Mon.-Fri.
Buses and trams - Prins Hendrikkade 108, tel: 551 49 11. 0830-1530 Mon.-Fri.
Trains - tel: 557 85 44. 0700-2200 Mon.-Sat.
Taxis - tel: 77 77 77.
Schiphol Airport - tel: 49 14 33.

Maatjes: Fresh young herrings caught between the months of May and July. At this time of year they are sold from street stalls, and you will see local people demonstrating the traditional way of eating them - hold them up by the tail, throw back your head and swallow hard!

Madurodam: A miniature city with working models situated in The Hague (see **A-Z**). Although many of the buildings are replicas of real buildings from various cities, the town as a whole is not based on any one existing place, but gives a general view of Dutch life. All kinds of vehicles move around the tiny streets, and there is even an accident scene. Attention to detail is superb throughout (the scale is 1:25), and Madurodam looks especially attractive under the night illuminations. See **CHILDREN**.

Magere Brug: A white, wooden swing bridge over the Amstel River (see **CANALS & RIVERS**) which is still operated by pulleys and is a favourite subject for holiday snaps.

Marken: 20 km from Amsterdam. Pop: 2000.
Formerly an isolated fishing community on an island in the Zuider Zee

(see **Markermeer**), Marken suffered badly from the enclosure of the sea in 1932 and turned to tourism to replace the lost income. The picturesque tarred houses on stilts and the traditional costumes which are still worn by the inhabitants have proved to be great attractions. Today only a causeway links the island to the mainland, but the proposed reclamation of land from the surrounding sea threatens to incorporate it fully into polder land. However, for the moment, Marken maintains its rather eccentric individuality. See EXCURSION 1.

Markermeer: The name given to that part of the IJsselmeer (see **A-Z**) enclosed in 1975 by the N 302 dike road from Enkhuizen to Lelystad. See EXCURSION 1.

Markets: Amsterdam has several lively and colourful street markets of all kinds where bargains are to be had for locals and visitors alike. For general goods, try the Flea Market (see **A-Z**), Westerstraat, Albert Cuypstraat or Nieuwmarkt. Antique lovers will enjoy the markets at Looiersgracht 38 and Elandsgracht 109, while bookworms should investigate Oudemanhuispoort. See CHURCHES, **Drijvende Bloemenmarkt**, **Opening Times**.

Metro: The underground system in Amsterdam is primarily a suburban commuter service, but it does provide the tourist with an alternative means of reaching the Jewish Quarter (see CITY DISTRICTS). Payment is by the *strippenkaart* system (see **Transport**).

Money: See **Banks**, **Credit Cards**, **Currency**, **Opening Times**, **Traveller's Cheques**.

Munttoren: Situated on the Muntplein (see SQUARES), the Munttoren was built by Hendrick de Keyser (see **Architecture**) on the remains of an ancient city gate. In 1672, 50 years after its construction, the tower was temporarily used as the local mint at a time when the French army occupied Utrecht (see **A-Z**), which housed the existing mint. It has since retained the name which derives from its function at that time. See MONUMENTS.

Leidseplein

Music: Whatever your taste in music, you will find something to your liking at any time of the year in one of Amsterdam's numerous venues. On a less formal level, there are also buskers and street entertainers in all the city's major squares during the summer. See **CHURCHES**, **DISCOS**, **THEATRE & CINEMA 1**, **Concertgebouw**, **Festivals and Events**.

Nature: Amsterdam is justifiably proud of its extensive parkland and greenery. Amid all the hustle and bustle of the city you are never far from a quiet park in which to get away from it all. The Amsterdamse Bos (see **PARKS**) to the south east is a large woodland area which was specially designed to provide employment for the victims of the 1920s' depression. For animal lovers, there is Artis Zoo (see **CHILDREN**), which provides a wonderful natural environment for its animals. Outside the city there is a bird sanctuary at Alphen aan de Rijn (see **A-Z**) and an ape sanctuary at Apeldoorn in Gelderland. Texel, an island 85 km north of Amsterdam, is the best location for bird-watching. It can be reached by ferry from Den Helder.

Newspapers and Magazines: The Dutch national dailies include *De Telegraaf*, *Het Parool*, and *De Volkskrant*. The *Holland Herald* is published monthly in English and features news and listings. Another useful what's-on publication is *Amsterdam This Week*, issued by the

VVV (see **Tourist Information**). The major international newspapers and periodicals are widely available, and British papers appear on the day of publication.

Nightlife: Most Amsterdammers tend to eat early. Dinner at home is usually over by 1930, leaving the evening free for going to the theatre or cinema, or having a few drinks. Bars close around midnight or 0100, when business starts to pick up in the discos. The Red Light District (see **CITY DISTRICTS, WALK 4, A-Z**), with its peep-shows, sex shops and seedy clubs, is one of the busiest areas for nightlife. Topless bars are to be found on Thorbeckeplein. See **CAFÉS, DISCOS, MODERN BARS, RESTAURANTS, THEATRE & CINEMA, Gambling, Leidseplein, Rembrandtsplein**.

Opening Times: These inevitably vary, but generally:
Banks - 0900-1600 Mon.-Wed. & Fri., 0900-1900 Thurs.
Post Offices - 0830-1800 Mon.-Wed. & Fri., 0830-2030 Thurs., 0900-1200 Sat.
VVV (Tourist Information Service) - 0900-1900 daily (Nov.-Mar.); 0845-2300 Mon.-Sat., 1000-1730 Sun. (Apr.-Oct.).
Museums - 1000-1700 Tues.-Sat., 1300-1700 Sun.
Shops - 1300-1800 Mon., 0900-1800 Tues., Wed. & Fri., 0900-2100 Thurs., 0900-1700 Sat.
Markets - 0900-1600 Mon.-Sat.
Cafés/Bars - 1000-0100 daily.

Orientation: The centre of Amsterdam is bounded to the north by Centraal Station (see **OFFICIAL BUILDINGS**), where many tram and bus routes terminate. The main thoroughfares of Nieuwezijds Voorburgwal and Damrak run south from here through Dam Square (see **SQUARES, A-Z**), Damrak becoming Rokin at this point. The southern ends of these streets lie in Spui and Muntplein (see **SQUARES**). To the east are the Red Light District (see **CITY DISTRICTS, WALK 4, A-Z**), the old town, and the Jewish Quarter (see **CITY DISTRICTS**), which are intersected by the Oudezijds Voorburgwal, Oudezijds Achterburgwal, Geldersekade, Kloveniersburgwal and Oudeschans (all running roughly north to south). The main canals (see **CANALS & RIVERS, A-Z**) form two-thirds of a horseshoe shape, enclosing these areas on their western and southern sides. The Jordaan (see **CITY DISTRICTS**, **WALK 1**, **A-Z**) lies further to the west on the other side of the canals, while the Museumplein district (see **CITY DISTRICTS**, **SQUARES**) and the fashionable Old South are to the south of the city centre, also across the canals.

Parking: Searching for a parking space in Amsterdam can be a frustrating experience. Metered bays (which charge reasonable rates) are to be found on many of the side streets, but they are usually occupied from early in the morning and double parking is quite common. Illegally parked cars run the risk of being towed away and a hefty fine is payable for recovery. There is a multi-storey car park on Marnixstraat beside the police station.

Passports: For visits of up to three months, nationals from EC countries, North America and the Antipodes require only a valid passport to enter the Netherlands. Other nationals may also require a visa.

Pedalos: See **Canal Bike Hire**.

Petrol: There are fewer places to buy petrol in Amsterdam than in many other major cities, but you will find numerous modern service stations outside the city. Prices do not vary significantly from the rest of western Europe.

Pets: All cats and dogs must be vaccinated, except those from Belgium and Luxembourg. You must be able to produce a vaccination certificate issued by a recognized veterinary authority.

Police: Although the police are armed and have adopted a higher profile in recent years (in order to clamp down on the drug problem), they generally have a laid-back attitude and are extremely approachable. See **Crime and Theft**, **Emergencies**, **Lost and Found**.

Post Office: The head post office is at Nieuwezijds Voorburgwal 182 (see **OFFICIAL BUILDINGS**), and there are smaller branches in all parts of the city. You can also buy stamps at postcard kiosks and from slot machines. Parcels are handled by the Postkantoor, Oosterdok 3-5. See **Opening Times**.

Public Holidays: 1 Jan.; Easter Monday; 30 Apr.; Ascension Day (usually in early May); Whit Monday (mid-May); 25-26 Dec.

Public Toilets: Few and far between, but the standard is high and normally includes provision for the disabled. *Heren* for men and *Damen* for women. Some have an attendant (who may expect a tip), but otherwise facilities are generally free.

Railways: A modern, efficient railway system links Amsterdam to all parts of the Netherlands and the rest of the Continent. Services within the city largely cater for suburban travel. Ticket prices are moderate, and reduced fares are available for regular travellers. Centraal Station is Amsterdam's main railway station (see **OFFICIAL BUILDINGS**).

Red Light District: Concentrated in that part of the old town surrounding the northern ends of Oudezijds Voorburgwal and Oudezijds Achterburgwal, the notorious Red Light District exerts a fascination for even the most staid of Amsterdam's visitors. The buildings of genuine historical interest like the Oude Kerk (see **CHURCHES**) and the excellent Amstelkring Museum (see **MUSEUMS 2**) seem incongruous among the gaudy sights of lurid sex shops and prostitutes seated in the windows. The area is known by the locals as the *Walletjes* (Little Walls), and the affectionate name conveys the sense of good-natured wickedness that pervades the district. The atmosphere is a little more intimidating by day as drug addicts and pushers tend to hang around, but when the clubs open at night and the streets become crowded you can wander around quite safely, taking in the remarkable sights. See **CITY DISTRICTS**, **WALK 4**.

Religious Services: the following are held on Sundays:
Reformed Churches: Westerkerk, Prinsengracht 281 (1030).
                      Oude Kerk, Oudekerksplein 23 (1100).
                      Engelse Kerk, Begijnhof 48 (1030 - in English).
                      Church of England, Groenburgwal 42 (1030).
Roman Catholic: Begijnhofkerk, Begijnhof 29 (1200 - in English).
                      De Papegaai, Kalverstraat 58 (0900, 1045, 1215).
                      St Nicolaaskerk, Prins Hendrikkade 73 (1100).

Rembrandt (1606-69): Rembrandt Harmensz van Rijn was born in Leiden (see **A-Z**) and studied painting from an early age. Settling in Amsterdam in 1631, he embarked on an artistic career which was to establish him as the Netherlands' most famous painter, and, in many people's minds, its best. His reputation was established with *The Anatomical Lesson* in 1632 (see **Waag**). In 1642 he produced the famous

Night Watch, which was not highly regarded at the time, but nowadays is accepted as his masterpiece. It is one of the glories of the Rijksmuseum (see **MUSEUMS 1**, **A-Z**), where many of his paintings and sketches are housed. More of his works can be seen in his former home Het Rembrandthuis (see **MUSEUMS 3**). Rembrandt died in poverty.

Rembrandtsplein: Situated near the northern reaches of the Amstel River (see **CANALS & RIVERS**) and the Muntplein (see **SQUARES**), the Rembrandtsplein is one of Amsterdam's lively nightlife centres. A statue of the great painter (see **A-Z**) stands in the centre, and restaurants, bars, strip clubs and cinemas border the square, which bustles with noise and activity at night. The most notable building in the vicinity is the remarkable Tuschinski Cinema (see **MONUMENTS**, **THEATRE & CINEMA 1**, **WALK 5**). See **SQUARES**.

Restaurants: Although not renowned as a gourmet's paradise, Amsterdam does have a wide range of restaurants to suit all tastes and pockets. Many are clustered round Leidseplein and Rembrandtsplein (see **SQUARES**, **A-Z**). As a consequence of the Netherlands' imperial past there are numerous Indonesian and Surinamese restaurants, while other ethnic cuisines available include Cantonese, Japanese, Indian, Creole, Pakistani, and Greek. Look out for the Tourist Menu sign in restaurant windows. It indicates that inexpensive three-course set meals are available. The familiar international fast-food chains are all represented. In a budget category restaurant a three-course meal (not including wine) could come to less than f25 a head; f25-f50 can be considered moderate; expensive establishments will set you back upwards of f50. See **RESTAURANTS**, **Food**.

Rijksmuseum: Designed by P. J. H. Cuypers (see **Architecture**) in the 1880s, this neo-Gothic building did not meet with great favour at the time of its construction. It is colossal and demands a visit of at least several hours to do justice to the magnificent art treasures it contains. Exhibits include ceramics, glassware, silverware, textiles and even dolls' houses, but the main attraction is the collection of paintings, and in particular the works of Rembrandt (see **A-Z**), Franz Hals and Vermeer

Rijksmuseum

(see **A-Z**). There are also displays of Asian and Islamic art, 18th and 19thC paintings, and sculptures of all kinds. The ground floor contains historical exhibits relating to the Netherlands dating from medieval times to the Second World War. See **MUSEUMS 1**.

Rotterdam: 80 km from Amsterdam. Pop: 555,000.
Europe's biggest port, Rotterdam sits on a vast estuary formed by the rivers Maas and Rhine. Few old buildings survived the bombing raids of the Second World War and the city has virtually been rebuilt since then, its seafaring heritage having greatly influenced the architecture of the modern buildings. The harbour is one of the busiest in the world and can be seen by boat on a guided tour which will take you inside the docks. There is a panoramic view of the port from the Euromast, at Parkhaven 20, but only for those with a head for heights. The Boymans-van Beuningen Museum at Mathenesserlaan 18-20 has a fine collection of Dutch paintings, including works by Hieronymus Bosch, Pieter Brueghel, Peter Paul Rubens (see **A-Z**) and Rembrandt (see **A-Z**).

Royal Palace: The grandeur of the Koninklijk Paleis belies the fact that when it was built, in the mid-17thC, it was only intended as the Stadhuis or Town Hall. Such ostentation was only possible in the Golden Age. So magnificent is the building that the Emperor Louis Napoleon chose it for his palace in 1808. Today the Dutch royal family uses the palace only occasionally and it serves as a museum when they are not in residence. The entrance is hard to find behind the seven arches embellishing the facade and the story goes that the doorway was made as unobtrusive as possible to protect the Stadhuis from attack. The interiors are works of art in themselves, with majestic pillars, ornate carvings and lavish decorations and furnishings adorning the Council Room, Throne Room and Royal Apartments. It is conveniently located on Dam Square (see **SQUARES, A-Z**) in the heart of the city. See **MUSEUMS 1, OFFICIAL BUILDINGS, WALK 2**.

Rubens, Sir Peter Paul (1577-1640): Painter born in Siegen in Westphalia where his father was exiled. The bourgeois Rubens family lived there in a state of poverty, but still managed to give their son a good education in Antwerp. From an early age he could speak Flemish, French, German and Latin, and at 14 he began to study painting. In 1600 he travelled round Italy, which greatly influenced his later work and where he met Monteverdi and Galileo. Returning to Antwerp in 1608, he continued his career as a painter of cathedral frescoes, although he was also much valued for his skills as a diplomat. He died leaving over 2000 works, some of which are housed in the Mauritshuis in The Hague (see **A-Z**) and the Boymans-van Beuningen Museum in Rotterdam (see **A-Z**).

Schreierstoren: This ancient monument stands near Centraal Station (see **OFFICIAL BUILDINGS**) at the north end of the Geldersekade. It was originally part of the ancient fortifications that protected the city, and once overlooked the sea (before the modern-day expansion of the harbour). Legend has it that this was the spot where the women of Amsterdam gathered to wave tearful farewells to their husbands as they set off on voyages of exploration during the Middle Ages. The name means 'Tower of Tears'. See **MONUMENTS, WALK 4**.

Koninklijk Paleis

Schreierstoren

Shopping: Some of the main shopping areas are:
Kalverstraat - a pedestrianized street with a variety of shops of all sizes.
Pieter Cornelisz Hooftstraat/Beethovenstraat/Van Baerlestraat - up-market shops selling designer clothes and quality goods.
Runstraat/Huidenstraat - unusual small boutiques and gift shops.
Spiegelgracht/Nieuwe Spiegelstraat - works of art, antiques, gifts.
See **SHOPPING**, **Best Buys**, **Souvenirs**.

Souvenirs: Plain and painted wooden clogs of all sizes are sold in many gift shops and are a popular present. Imitation Delftware is also common, and is considerably cheaper than the genuine article - small items cost only a few guilders (see **Delft**). Cigars are so inexpensive that they also make ideal gifts for smokers (see **Cigarettes and Tobacco**). Other popular souvenirs include dolls in traditional costume and model windmills. See **SHOPPING**, **Best Buys**, **Shopping**.

Sports: As you would expect in a major city, Amsterdam has facilities for the popular participatory sports such as tennis, squash, swimming and golf. Cycling (see **Bicycles**), ice-skating (see **Leidseplein**), and sailing (see **Boat Hire**) are particularly associated with the Netherlands. For those who prefer to spectate, there is motor-racing at Zandvoort (see **A-Z**), or football just about anywhere. The biggest local team is the famous Ajax Amsterdam, whose stadium is in the east of the city at Middenweg 401. The ground is small so tickets for important matches must be reserved well in advance. See **PARKS**.

Stedelijk Museum: Amsterdam's foremost collection of modern and contemporary art is housed in this neo-Renaissance building, dating from the 1890s, in the Museumplein (see **SQUARES**). There are frequent temporary exhibitions, so check in the entrance hall to find out what is currently on offer. Amongst the permanent exhibits, you will find works by Picasso, Van Gogh, Chagall, Cezanne, Matisse and Monet. The museum also focuses on the De Stijl, the group of artists, architects, and designers of the 1920s and 30s whose major figures included Piet Mondriaan and Gerrit Rietveld (see **Architecture**). American pop art is also well represented. See **MUSEUMS 1, WALK 3**.

Street Numbers: In times gone by houses were not identified by numbers but by the insignia displayed on their facades, often depicting the owner's trade. Many of these can still be seen today. The Amsterdams Historisch Museum (see **MUSEUMS 2**) has a collection of such house heraldries, the oldest of which dates back to 1603 and portrays a milkmaid. This tradition continues today in some quarters: for instance there is a sculpted welding hammer dating from 1973 poised above a welder's door on Oudelbrakstraat. The Emperor Louis Napoleon introduced street numbers in 1806, and they follow the conventional system of even and odd numbers on opposite sides of the street. In addresses, the number follows the street name.

Tasting Houses: These drinking houses, known as *proeflokaals*, are singular to Amsterdam. Originally they were the sampling houses of the *jenever* distilleries (see **Drinks**), where customers could taste their products before purchasing the bottle of their choice, but now off-sales are prohibited. Pop in and enjoy some of the many varieties of *jenever* on offer. Their decor is usually cheerful but basic, with no tables or chairs.

Taxis: You cannot hail taxis in the street, but there are many taxi ranks near railway stations and in busy public areas. Tel: *77 77 77* to order a cab - the service is usually quick and efficient, but rather expensive. Service charge is included in the metered fare, but it is customary to add a small tip. See **Tipping**.

Telephones: There is no shortage of modern, well-maintained call boxes. They take 25ct and f1 coins, and most display a guide in English explaining how to operate them. Many cafés and hotels have older call boxes which take only 25ct coins. The Telehuis at Raadhuisstraat 48 is open 24 hr for long-distance calls. Payment is made at the desk after the call is completed.

To phone abroad, first dial 07. When you hear a change in the dialling tone, add the appropriate international code (*eg* UK 44, USA 01), followed by the area code (if an initial 0 normally occurs here, it should be omitted). Then add the rest of the number.

Television and Radio: The three Hilversum (see **A-Z**) radio stations broadcast a variety of different music programmes, and there are three Dutch television channels which all show undubbed American and British films and series. French films are also often broadcast. British and Continental television and radio stations are easily received with good equipment. Some areas also have cable TV.

Time Differences: Central European Time, which is followed in the Netherlands during the winter months, is ahead of Greenwich Mean Time by one hour. Clocks are put forward by one hour in summer. Therefore, Amsterdam is always an hour ahead of the UK and six ahead of East Coast USA.

Tipping: A service charge is normally included in hotel and restaurant bills, but it is customary also to leave a few coins (f3-f5). Hotel porters expect f2 per bag, while tour guides and taxi drivers expect 5-10% of the fare.

Tourist Information: The Netherlands Tourist Information Service is known as the VVV (pronounced Vay-Vay-Vay), and their offices bear this logo in blue. In Amsterdam you will find them at Stationsplein 10 and Leidsestraat 106. As well as providing general information, the VVV will exchange currency, book hotels (for a small fee), issue Museumcards (see **Budget**), and organize excursions, car rental, *etc.* Their offices are generally busy so expect queues.

Tours and Excursions: Amsterdam, known as the Venice of the North, actually has more canals than Venice and is best seen by boat. There are many tours to choose from, each offering basically the same service, so just opt for the most convenient. Embarkation points are on Prins Hendrikkade, Rokin and Damrak. Boat trips usually last one hour and depart every 15 min. More luxurious (and more expensive) dinner cruises, lasting three or four hours, are available in the evenings. City coach tours are also popular. For example, you can enjoy a three-hour trip round Dam (see **SQUARES**, **A-Z**), some of the famous bridges, the Rijksmuseum (see **MUSEUMS 1**, **A-Z**) and a diamond factory. There are also specialist tours of museums, diamond factories and other sights of particular interest. A recently-introduced service is the Museum Boat, which departs daily from the Noord-Zuid Hollands Koffie Huis near Centraal Station (see **OFFICIAL BUILDINGS**) at 0930, and visits nine main museums (costs f7,50). Company representatives tout for business along the busy thoroughfares like Damrak, offering inexpensive coach trips to major cities like The Hague, Rotterdam and Utrecht (see **A-Z**) and other attractions such as the tulip fields (see **EXCURSION 3**, **A-Z**) or the wind-mill country (see **Zaanse Schans**).

Trams: Most of the centre of Amsterdam, and some areas further afield, are served by trams. They are one of the city's most distinctive sights, and a fast and convenient method of getting around. Payment is by the *strippenkaart* fare system (see **Transport**).

Transport: Schiphol Airport is 15 km from Amsterdam (see **Airport**). Buses, trains and the Metro provide regular services between here and Centraal Station (see **OFFICIAL BUILDINGS**). There are also taxi ranks. The journey takes about 15 min.
Buses, trams and the Metro use a fare system known as *strippenkaart*. These tickets can be bought in advance at post offices, railway stations and some shops, and consist of two, three, ten or 15 strips which the passenger must cancel according to the number of fare zones included in the journey (two strips for one zone, three strips for two zones, *etc*). Ticket inspections are very frequent to deter abuse of the system. More economical daily or weekly tickets which allow unlimited travel are

available from the transport office on the Stationsplein (approx. f9 and f25 respectively). See **Buses**, **Metro**, **Railways**, **Taxis**, **Trams**.

Traveller's Cheques: Not all hotels accept traveller's cheques in payment. They can be readily exchanged at banks and *bureaux de change*. See **Banks**, **Opening Times**.

Tulips: Tulip bulbs were first brought to the Netherlands by sailors returning from Turkey around1600. The name is thought to originate from the Turkish *tulband,* meaning 'turban'. A chemist named Wulich Kierwertz is credited with installing the first window box containing tulips. Within 50 years the flowers were popular all over the Netherlands and by 1634 tulip bulbs were being quoted on the Stock Exchange. The business expanded so much over the next few years that bulbs cost as much as f4400 each. In 1637 the government stepped in and prices dropped, causing many investors to go bankrupt (including the famous painter Jan Van Goyen). Today the main tulip-growing areas lie to the south west of Amsterdam. See **EXCURSION 3**, **Aalsmeer**, **Best Buys**, **Drijvende Bloemenmarkt**, **Haarlem**, **Keukenhof**.

Utrecht: 38 km from Amsterdam. Pop: 230,000.
This city, the fourth largest in the Netherlands, played a major role in the ecclesiastical history of the country. Its surviving religious buildings constitute the city's main attractions (there are numerous churches and convents, many of great antiquity) as much of the modern city is rather unprepossessing. The Domtoren (Cathedral Tower) on Domplein is the most outstanding building in old Utrecht and dates from the 13thC. Climb it for excellent views of the city. Amongst the few museums to visit is the Music Box and Barrel Organ Museum at Achter de Dom 12, which is a real curiosity.

Van Gogh Museum: Opened in 1973, this modern building was designed by Gerrit Rietveld (see **Architecture**) and houses the private collection of Theo Van Gogh, brother of the great and troubled artist, Vincent. The museum sets out to give a complete insight into the life and character of the man as well as his work. Letters and documents are exhibited, as well as articles written about Van Gogh and examples of his influence on his contemporaries and on the art world in general. However, the central core of the collection consists of over 200 paintings and 500 drawings by Vincent himself. See **MUSEUMS 1, WALK 3**.

Vermeer, Jan (1632-75): A native of Delft (see **A-Z**) and a contemporary of Rembrandt (see **A-Z**), Vermeer is recognized now, if not during his own lifetime, as one of the great painters of the Golden Age. Few details about his life are known, perhaps because his Catholicism required him to maintain a low profile. Precision and detail are the hallmarks of his work. His output was not prodigious, but some of his most notable paintings can be seen in the Rijksmuseum in Amsterdam (see **MUSEUMS 1, A-Z**), and in the Mauritshuis in The Hague (see **A-Z**).

Volendam: 18 km from Amsterdam. Pop: 17,000.
A small port on the Markermeer (see **A-Z**) which, like so many others, had to turn to tourism to replace the income once generated by fishing that was lost by the enclosure of the Zuider Zee (see **IJsselmeer, Markermeer**). Visitors flock to see the harbour and the local people bedecked in their colourful traditional costumes. See **EXCURSION 1**.

Vondelpark: In the1960s Amsterdam's main city-centre park attracted droves of flower people and hippies. Today it retains some of the same free-and-easy atmosphere. All kinds of open-air entertainments go on here during the summer, both theatrical and musical, impromptu and prearranged. Its sports facilities are also good, and the park houses the interesting Nederlands Filmmuseum (see **MUSEUMS 3**). See **PARKS**.

Waag: Situated in Nieuwmarkt, the Waag (Weigh-house) is a remnant of the old city wall and has many interesting corners to explore. It was once used by various local guilds: the Surgeons' Guild dissected the bodies of executed criminals here, as Rembrandt's famous painting *The Anatomical Lesson* records (see **A-Z**). The Waag formerly housed the Amsterdams Historisch and Joods Historisch museums (see **MUSEUMS 2**).

What's On: The best way to keep up with the latest shows, concerts,

Zaanse Schans

events and exhibitions is to buy the listings periodical *Amsterdam This Week*, published by the VVV. See **Tourist Information**.

Youth Hostels: To stay in youth hostels in the Netherlands you must possess an international Y H card. If you do not already have one, it can be obtained from Nederlandse Jeugdherberg, Prof. Tulpplein 4, 1018 GX Amsterdam, tel: 26 44 33. The charge is f35. Youth hostels cost approx. f18 per night including breakfast.

Zaandam: 10 km from Amsterdam. Pop: 6900.
This industrial suburb to the north west of the city is notable for its association with Tsar Peter the Great of Russia, who came here several times to study local shipbuilding methods for which the town was famous. The house he stayed in is open to visitors. See **EXCURSION 2**.

Zaanse Schans: A reconstruction of a 17th-18thC windmill village, built in 1960 and located 12 km from Amsterdam, outside Zaandam (see **A-Z**). Here you can explore various antiquities museums, visit old-style houses and shops, and watch craftsmen working at their various trades. The numerous windmills contribute to the town's picturesque appeal. See **EXCURSION 2**.

Zandvoort: 30 km from Amsterdam. Pop: 16,000.
A seaside resort to the west of Amsterdam, with miles of beaches fringed by cafés and restaurants. To the north is the motor-racing circuit which hosts the Dutch Formula One Grand Prix. See **EXCURSION 2**.

Zuider Zee: See **IJsselmeer**, **Markermeer**.